Miracle Motors

A Pert Near True Story

Peggy Senger Morrison

Unction Press

Published by Unction Press
710 Thompson NE, Salem, OR 97301
United States of America

First Edition July 2014
Second Edition March 2015

ISBN: 978-0-9819989-3-0

Portions of this book have been previously published by Peggy Senger Parsons. This title contains material from: Extreme Unction - Christ and the Lure of the Open Road (1998), So There I Was (2009), and So There I was in Africa (2009). Portions have also appeared on Peggy's blogs at sillypoorgospel.blospot.com, unction.org and ReligionandSpirituality.com, a publication of United Press International. All scripture quotes are King James Version or paraphrases by the author. Additional quotations appear from: The adventures of Don Quixote by Miguel De Cervantes; The Adventures of Huck Finn, Mark Twain; The Serenity Prayer, attributed to Reinhold Neibuhr; He Giveth More Grace - Annie Flint and Hubert Mitchell; and Martin Luther, Letter 99, Saemmtliche Schriften. The Lily Tomlin quote was written by Jane Wagner for Lily Tomlin's stage performances. The prayer recited by Marcile Crandall in "A Blessing" is a paraphrase of a prayer for protection and peace commonly used by The Church of England.

Cover design and interior artwork by Brandon Buerkle
http://www.brandonbuerkle.com/

For Nia Grace Cline and all the girls of the 21st century.

Contents

Maps

Oregon 3
The American West 4
Africa 6

Prologue

Unmediated 8
Pert Near True 11

Part I:
Roots and Wings

My Mother's Dream 16
Don't Tell Your Mother 19
Apostate 23
Mario 26
Mercy and Goodness 28
Surrender 30
Wrack and Ruin 33
Rebel 35
Failure 37
Rocinante 41

Part 2:
Shiny Side Up, Rubber Side Down

How I got to Scotts Mills 46
Running 50
Quakers 54
Subversive 56
Weather 59
Crooked 61
Talking 63
Traction 65
Escape 68
When the Bad Thing Happens 72
Stopping 75
Righteous Revolution 77
Reconciliation 79

Part 3:
Deep in the Heart of Texas

The Annunciation 88
Prepare Ye the Way 90
Horse and Rider 92
It's not Heavy, It's My Luggage 94
Anticipation 96
A Blessing 98
On the First Day 100
Dancing With the Angels, While the Lions Roar 102
Providence, Nevada 107
Sabbath 112
Samurai Road Warriors 114
Cats from the Freeway 117
Born To Be Mild 124
Real Men Marry Preachers 128
Davy Crockett: King of the Wild Frontier 130
Doing It 132
Our Lady of Junction 134
I Heard the Approach of Four Horsemen 137

The Land of Enchantment 140
Rocky Mountain High 145
Driving like Jehu 147

PART 4:
SAYS WHO?

Bucephalus 154
The Scariest Day 157
The Missionary Position 160
Powerless 163
In Bujumbura 169
Gitega 173
Inclusion 177
When a Schism is not a Schism 180
Left Behind 183
Dark 185
Healing 187
Groups 189
Of Bits and Governors 193
Sin 196
Love—Insistent, Persistent and Militant 200

PART 5:
WAY OPENS WIDE

Madame Moto-Muzungu 206
The WAY of Traffic 212
Glory or Death 215
Subversion—African Edition 216
Providence, Burundi 219
Service 222
Subversion—Shopping Edition 223
Celebrity 225

PART 6:
OFF THE GRID

Fresh Roads 232
Mechanical Failure 235
Forest Fires 238
Gas Anxiety 241
Chick Bike 244
Begging 247
Lost 252
Vocation 257
Nose to the Barn 259

EPILOGUE

Ab Aterno 264

Gratitudes

This work started in 1998 as a motorcycle travelogue. I am grateful to Marge Abbott for pushing me to write that first story. I appreciate Bob Rodriguez of the Illinois Valley News and Larry Moffitt of United Press International for insisting that I could keep my own voice while teaching me to trust editors, a least a little. About half of this book has been previously published in some form.

As the 15 year anniversary of the Texas ride rolled around I decided to re-print and enlarge that story. Deep gratitude to the editor of this book, Katharine Hyzy, for challenging me to make it much bigger than that, and for calling me to a level of honesty that I would not achieved on my own. Thanks to Brandon Buerkle for the amazing art, and Audrey for catching the errors. Special thanks to Bill Zuelke for walking with me–you hold up a mirror that regularly startles me into deeper faith. For my children who keep me honest, and for Alivia who keeps me sane. I am grateful for angels who stay close and for a God who talks.

May this work be useful to the Truth.

Peggy Senger Morrison
Salem, Oregon, Summer 2014

Maps

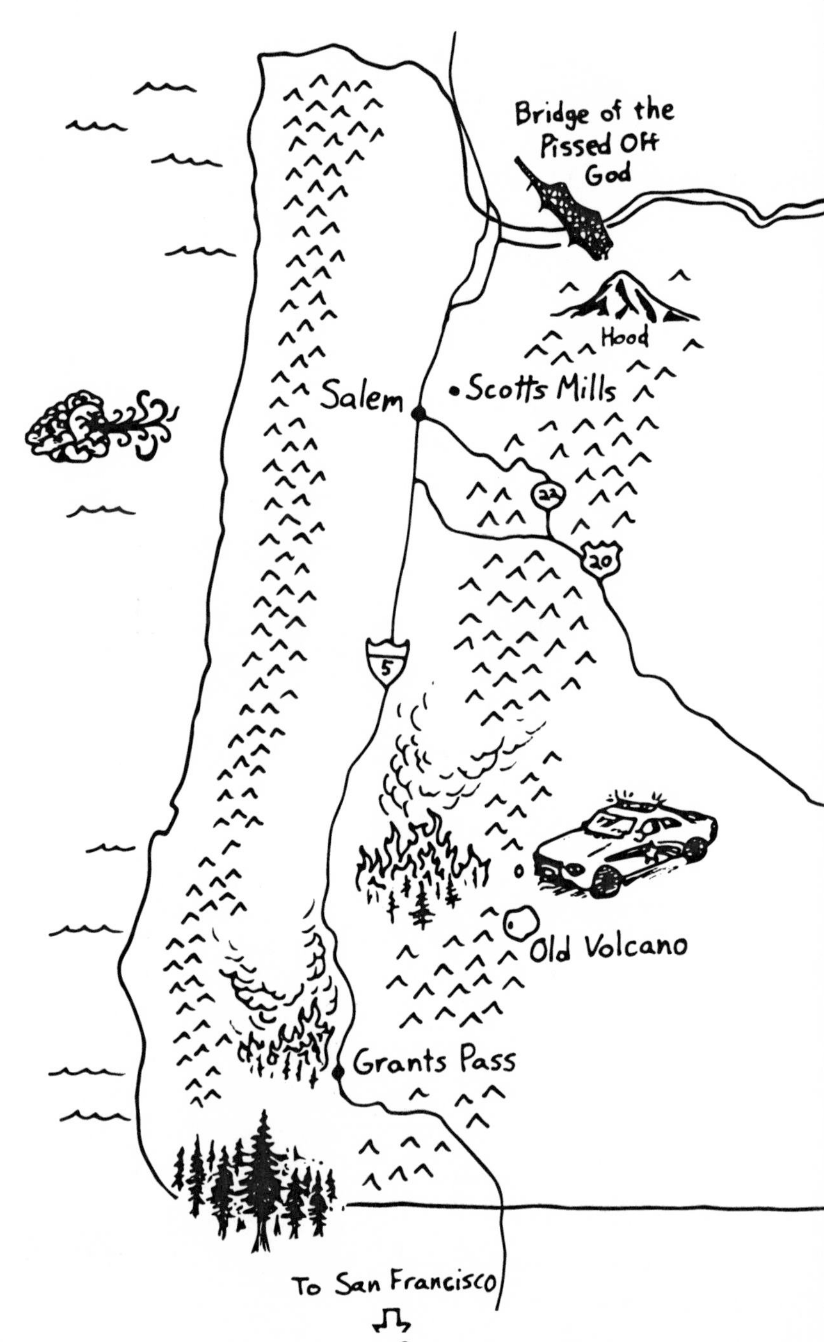
Bridge of the Pissed Off God
Hood
Salem
Scotts Mills
22
20
5
Old Volcano
Grants Pass
To San Francisco

OREGON
84
Chief Joseph
95
LOST
Snake River
Gouge Eye Saloon
20
Burns
20
78
Out of Gas
Basque Country
Pie
95

The American West

Providence
Moab
Elvisville
Mancos Pass
Pueblo
Hoover Dam
Big Ditch
Babylon
The Midwest
Santa Fe
R.I.P. Kid
Bake
Broil
Lordsburg
Roswell
El Paso
Sweetwater
Eden
Our Lady of Junction
The Alamo
Warm Ocean

Africa

PROLOGUE

Unmediated

My friend Owen rides a smart-looking, flat bench, Triumph Bonneville. He will not ruin the looks of it with an aftermarket windscreen. He wears an open face helmet. Usually, he doesn't even wear glasses. I regularly opine that this is foolish, and relate that every time I get hit in the face shield with a rock I tell myself that I just saved my face. He says, "I've been hit by a rock—I say... Ouch!" If we didn't have a helmet law, Owen probably wouldn't wear his lid. Owen rides for the feel of riding. We all do, to varying degrees.

When you trade in your car for a motorcycle, you are trading in your buffer zone. People get motion sick in cars because your eyes tell your brain that you are moving very fast and your butt thinks you are sitting in an easy chair. There is no such confusion on a bike. Every part of you understands what is going on.

You can daydream while driving a car. Some people do that on motorcycles, but then they die. Riding requires awareness. You can drive a car mildly inebriated. It is a bad idea, but it can be done. It is a much worse idea on a bike.

On the bike, you don't just smell the occasional skunk. You smell a field of mint vs. a field of corn. You smell the rain before it comes.

In the car, you have a gauge to tell you if the engine is hot. On the bike, the engine is between your legs and you can take its temperature anytime. You also feel the ambient temperature change in a shadowed dip or curve—like skimming through a pool. You feel the radiant heat of the sun on your head and back.

You can hear things you would never otherwise notice. The engine sounds of the traffic around you. You know that the rubber of your tires on the pavement sings a completely different tune when the road is hot or wet, smooth or coarse. And without the noise of a radio, or the conversation of a passenger, you hear your own internal voice. Sometimes you get quiet enough that even that voice turns off.

You feel more alive, in part, because you are aware that you are closer to death. This measured flirtation with mortality is known to every adventurer. It's not suicidal. You are directly engaged with your every sense of the world around you.

We bikers seek the unmediated experience of motor travel. The fullest experience possible. Between us and the world hurtling past, we allow only that which makes the experience bearable. I cannot bear it without a wind screen and helmet. I usually want my leathers. My friend Owen gets closer than I.

And so it is with the things of God. Some of us want and need the gauges that provide feedback on how we are doing. Some desire the guidance and direction of gurus and priests. Some seek out an owner's manual, or the relative safety and stability that comes with structure. Some hunger for the stories of the saints and heroes. Some build cathedrals and kivas to give place to faith, or score and breathe music to speak what is essentially unspeakable. All these things have value. All these things have fed and clothed souls for millennia. All these things are good.

And sometimes, some of us want to strip it all away and have an unmediated experience of God. We want to taste God, and smell God, and vibrate with, the presence of God. We want every part of us to know that we are moving towards, or even away, from grace. We welcome even the rock slap of reality that stings us into wakefulness. Our focus is forced, because having given up the buffer, we will die if we doze. And we wouldn't have it any other way.

Motorcyclists did not invent unmediated attentiveness, but they know it intimately. I am a Quaker. We did not invent unmediated theology, but at our best, it is what we practice. This is a story of an unmediated relationship with God, living with a vivid awareness of God's realm. It may be disguised as a memoir, but it is really a post-modern narrative theology. It is everything that I know by direct experience with God. It has more in common with the journals of the first Quakers and the confessions of old Catholics than it does with the systematic theologies of modern scholars. It also has more motorcycles.

Pert Near True

"Now look, your grace," said Sancho, "What you see over there aren't giants, but windmills, and what seems to be arms are just their sails, that go around in the wind and turn the millstone."

"Obviously," replied Don Quixote, "You don't know much about adventures."

-Don Quixote

Cowboy Poets have a lot of time to think. It makes them great philosophers. Cowboy Poets are also tied very closely to the real world of saddle sores and animal shit. This makes their wisdom practical. They are keen observers of the glories and cruelties of nature. There are not many Cowboy Poet atheists.

Motorcyclists and Cowboy Poets usually have something to talk about. If nothing else, they can talk about the weather. They can swap tales of long drives and busted rides. They are friends of solitude, but know how to take joy in the end of the trail. Everybody should know a Cowboy Poet.

My Cowboy Poet was known to speak up in Quaker meeting from time to time. He had the right cadence–serious, but simple. His hat was always off in the presence of his God, and it was the only time I ever saw him take his hat off. When he spoke, he stuck to the point and spoke what God put on his heart, and then sat down. He did tell stories-good ones.

One time, after meeting, I asked him if the rather fantastical story he had told was true. His answer was "Pert near." I laughed and asked him to explain pert near true. Quakers have a thing about truthfulness—we can be kind of persnickety about it. This has always made me a trifle uncomfortable. Then that good man changed my life with one sentence.

"Pert near true is a story that has so much truth to it, that it doesn't really matter whether it happened or not."

Wow—I do not think that old persnickety Quaker John Woolman would approve—he was a man who believed in the truth, the whole truth and nothing but the truth. I think Jesus of Nazareth and all his disciples knew this instinctively—they were a culture of story-tellers. But it was fresh revelation to me and solved so many problems.

You see, I was a childhood storyteller. Apparently a prevaricator. I don't remember when this started. I do know that it was a well-known fact by the time I was in grade school. One spring Sunday evening, when I was seven, a tree fell down in our backyard. It landed on top of my father's Ford Falcon and my grandfather's Rambler. It apparently did so quietly, because no one noticed as they sat in the living room eating my mother's pie and drinking coffee. I went out to the back porch to get my Sunday school missionary bank—it looked like a round African hut. The glue had been drying on its thatched roof and my mother had put it out of the kitchen.

The sight of the crushed automobiles was stunning. But only momentarily, and then I went screaming into the house, full-tilt News Flash into the midst of the adults. No one even set down their coffee. My father smiled indulgently. My grandmother frowned. My mother said "Peggy, now is not a good time for stories." No one even considered the possibility that I might be telling the truth. I do not remember who finally corroborated my scoop. I do remember that no one thought to apologize for not taking me seriously. I guess my reputation was just that entrenched even then.

Eventually I developed an ethic for truthfulness. I am a Quaker because I need to be one, not because I am naturally inclined.

But I never stopped telling stories. I learned to tell good stories to illustrate spiritual truths. And God, in God's ironic wisdom, has seen fit to give me a life full of vivid, unusual, and occasionally incredible experiences. For a while, I worried a great deal about historicity. Then I relaxed into the doctrine of pert near true. Being a preacher of the pert near true doesn't mean making stuff up. It certainly precludes prevarication for personal profit or manipulative agenda. It means that you get to tell your stories with God's own ludicrous liberty. You paint a scene like God paints a sunset—not worrying about if it looks real.

Everything in this book is pert near true. Almost all of it really happened. But that doesn't really matter.

Part I:
Roots and Wings

Oz makes no sense without Kansas. The Odyssey is a pretty good tale without the Iliad, but you are never going to understand why the Gods are so torqued off at Odysseus. No banana ever sprouted in the tundra and you can't transplant one there either. Where you came from may not completely determine where and what you are, but divorcing the two is never a good idea. Ideas and opinions and theologies also have birthplaces. Cowboy poets, storytellers and narrative theologians all know how important it is to start the story in just the right place.

Sigmund Freud knew it always starts with the mother…

My Mother's Dream

My mother had me genetically engineered to be the perfect pastor's wife. She did this with prayer, not science. She did not factor in mutation.

I come from serious, religious, Midwestern people. They were a part of the American phenomenon called the Holiness Movement. It started as the most optimistic of sects. The idea being, through surrender, intention, and the grace of God, your sins would get littler and farther apart and eventually you could get to a place where you didn't really want to sin at all anymore, and God would honor that desire with a miracle called sanctification, and the sinning would just stop.

What a great plan. Sadly, it tended to degenerate into long lists of things we didn't do, and the judging of the people who did do them—which last time I checked, was still a sin.

Not that we didn't have our share of colorful characters. One of my great-grandfathers was a hillbilly preacher who got 24 children out of three wives. My Grandma Hubbell was born when old Tyre Crawley was 76 years old, and she had two younger siblings! On the other side, my great-grandfather, Johan Fritz Senger, was a drunk and a scoundrel. But he was a good enough father that during the influenza epidemic, on a late fall, dicey-weather day in 1918, he rode his motorcycle into Pueblo, Colorado, trying to reach his son's funeral. He froze to death in the attempt. The obit was found in his pocket.

The women who put up with these men were stronger than they were. We do not lack life force.

I was uncorked during the winter of '57, a classic vintage. My hometown, the city of Chicago, was not known for its Holiness, except perhaps, for a few blocks around the famous Moody Bible Institute, which was dedicated to stopping evolution in it tracks. And to rolling back Rock and Roll—they were against that too.

My mother owed God—big time. She had been born into a parsonage and sent upstate by her tender but extremely conservative parents. She was beautiful and smart and musically gifted. They sent her to a school called The Christian Evangelistic Institute, because Moody was too lax. No, really. Her job was to sift the young preachers, test their mettle and choose the very best. She failed. She dated them all and couldn't stand to yoke herself to a one of them. And then she refused to slink back home to spinsterhood. She stayed in the city, got a job, and fell madly in love with my semi-heathen, roller skate dance champion of a father.

When he asked her for a date, she said, "Which church would you like to go to?" He lied and said, "I like so many of them, you choose." She did. And he gave up the skates, and settled happily into the Holiness movement, because my mother was there. My grandparents were skeptical, but they adjusted.

Meanwhile, my mother owed God a pastor's wife. She was pretty sure that God kept score of these kinds of things, so I, the second child and only daughter, was anointed. She didn't really tell me this, she just supplied the piano and voice lessons, made sure I knew how to take minutes at the Women's Missionary Society meetings, and sewed my modest clothing. It bothered her a little bit that I took after my father in the climbing of trees and delighting in fireworks, but she figured I would grow out of it.

When I was little, I wanted to be an astronaut. Then I saw a Mercury capsule and realized that The Right Stuff included being suicidal, and gave that up. No one told me that girls couldn't be astronauts. By the end of grade school, I had decided on politics and told my mother that I intended to be the first female president. She didn't say that girls couldn't be president, but she did take the opportunity to let me in on her dream for me. Scales fell from my eyes. I said that I would take it under consideration, and I started quietly plotting my escape.

Don't Tell Your Mother

> The down will be up; the first will be last.
>
> -Jesus

I have come to believe that one of the core disciplines of a spiritual life, and especially a Christian life, ought to be the subverting of dominant paradigms. Creating and maintaining paradigms is also holy work, but it tends to get too much emphasis. Good Faith always embraces the reality of this paradox. God gave us Light—which is, impossibly, both wave and particle—so we would know this.

Subversion gets the bad rap of destruction and ruin, which people fear, but the Latin root simply means to overturn from beneath, as in, "Before we plant the tomatoes we need to go out and subvert the soil a bit." Subversion is healthy. Any way of being and every important cause has a tendency to calcify and get rigid. Subversion is necessary to get air to the roots. Yet, subverters do not get very good press—even though it would be fair to describe Science itself as a series of righteous subversions.

I got all my early lessons in subversion from my father. Dad grew up the barely-watched son of a Depression-era widow. He lived on the streets of the western edge of Chicagoland in the 1920's. He ran with a gang of boys who lived like wild things in the natural forest preserves that ring the city. They stole dynamite blasting caps from construction sites to blow up rocks in the Des Plaines River. They built forts and burrowed deep into riverbanks. They were so tough that their initiation rite was to lie between the rails of the

Burlington Northern Freight line and let a train roll over them. When another gang of boys built a series of tunnels too close to theirs, they lit fires at all the entrances they could find to smoke them out. In the winter they skated on thin ice and sometimes fell through. They had various moneymaking scams, and sometimes even went to school. My dad learned Latin at Proviso East. He learned to be a natural botanist and geologist in the woods. He was a natural-born subverter.

I didn't hear any of those good stories about his childhood until I was grown, because my mother wouldn't let him tell us. She didn't want us getting ideas. Mother created and maintained the paradigms of health and safety and order. Our father completely supported her in those things—unless he was subverting them.

Dad knew all the best sledding hills in the Forest Preserves. I have great memories of him, belly-down on the Flexible Flyer, me clinging to his back, flying through trees, and nearly off of cliffs, gliding across frozen ponds. We crashed, we got up, shook off the snow and laughed. Mother wasn't there; the whole thing was a cabin fever, get-the-kids-out-of-my-hair-for-a-while intervention. She was in charge of the cocoa afterwards. "Don't tell your mother that the ice cracked just a little bit, the water was only a foot deep." This was the sort of thing I heard from my dad every so often. It didn't destroy her paradigm. It actually reminded us of the gravity of the thing, but it also let a little air into it.

Dad would tell you about which trees were good for climbing, and he would let you climb the trees a little higher. When he was working in the church bell tower once, he let me go out on the roof just a little. The view of my neighborhood was so grand from up there.

Then I heard my mother's voice from way down below somewhere. "Orville! Get that child down from there right now!" and he hauled me in and said, "Don't scare your mother, now." He respected her concern even when he didn't really share it. The smile on his face said, we don't scare her when she notices—when she wants to see a wave, be a wave—when she isn't looking, you can be a particle.

Dad would get his hands on fireworks that mother didn't approve of. He would watch us extra close, or make us watch him. He didn't want to have to explain lost fingers to her.

He was the Yin to her Yang. They voted in opposite political parties—ironically she was the Democrat. But he read me the Sunday funnies every week. His favorite was Pogo. I knew from him that Walt Kelly was publicly mocking Senator Joe McCarthy every Sunday morning.

He was the scientist; she was the religionist, who respected his intelligence and interests. You could ask either of them questions. Mother's answers were more certain. Father made sure that we had a house full of National Geographics. I was about eight when I came to him after Sunday school and said, "Dad, this Noah thing just doesn't work. The boat is too small and there are too many kinds of animals, and the polar bears and penguins would never make it to Mesopotamia."

He replied, "Honey, it's a very old story, and I'm sure it's close to true, but the polar bears and the penguins were safe on their ice floes, Noah only had to save the local animals.—But honey, don't tell your mother I said so." That was beyond subversion; that was the seed of a revolution.

Dad was also a storyteller. If we were on a Wisconsin vacation road and a sign said "Caution Falling Rock," he might launch into a long tale of a famous Indian chief, named Falling Rock, who was fabled thereabouts and occasionally got cranky with tourists. Mother would roll her eyes, but smiled at him with muted adoration. She worried that we might not be able to distinguish his mythos from her Gospel Truth. Pert near true was his paradigm, not hers. And yet, she gave us Santa Claus.

I do not know whose idea it was to take Grandma and Grandpa Hubbell to the Field Museum of Natural History. Must have been Dad's, but Mother should have known better. The Bible does not mention dinosaurs, you know. Their existence just might cause the weak-minded to think the Earth was a lot older than the prescribed six grand orbits. My Grandma's paradigm was Biblical literal–that's where my mom got it.

That day, my tiny Grandma walked up to a T-Rex named Sue and shook her finger at it and proclaimed in that booming rotunda, "YOU ARE NOT REAL!"

I swear Sue flinched. I whirled at the other adults. We were not shouting people. Mother had her hands over her face, and Dad and Grandpa were smiling with respectful amusement.

The men in my family loved their strong women. The whole panoply was right there for me: paradigm, doubt, subversion, certainty, tolerance, shame and pride. They were all good.

Apostate

I was a-trembling, because I'd got to decide, forever, betwixt two things, and I knowed it.

I studied a minute, sort of holding my breath, and then says to myself: "All right then, I'll go to hell."

- Huck Finn

It was the spring of my twelfth year; I was out in the back yard on a warm Sunday evening. I had just decided to become apostate.

One of the problems with this picture is that I was twelve, and knew what apostasy was: willing, full-knowing rebellion against God and God's faith, a change of loyalty, defection. This was the choice of Lucifer, the fallen one.

Another problem was that it was precisely what I wanted.

At that age, I looked a lot like Pippy Longstockings: skinny, straggly hair in two messy braids, tall for my age, pale and weak. But I had left a Sunday evening class that was supposed to be my preparation for baptism, and made a big decision. No Thanks. I'll work for any team but yours.

My rebellion was supported by three pillars; God's people, God's teaching and God.

Despite the fact that I had loving parents who walked their talk, they seemed to be an anomaly. The guy teaching my baptism class preached love, and beat his kids. The big-deal youth preacher down at Moody Bible Institute thought that the most important thing we could do as young Christians was to smash all our rock 'n roll. What was he thinking? My mother didn't let me have any rock.

There were people telling me that I should simultaneously worry about college and the end of the world, which was going to happen any minute. I remember one youth pastor who told us that no matter who we had sex with first (whatever sex was), in God's eyes, we were married to that person for life, even if we repented and then married a Christian. These people seemed bad or nuts—take your pick.

Doctrine-wise, I had picked up this: "Hey little girl, the best person who ever lived was brutally murdered, and it was your fault." Nobody in our church ever debated whether to blame the Jews or the Romans. Those nails were meant for your hands, and the guy with the hammer is just part of the plan. This was a bit heavy for a child.

And then there was my personal observation of God. He apparently stood by while the world was in a severe mess. His supposed cure on the cross did not seem to have had much affect. And I did not buy the notion that this was also our fault for not accepting Jesus as our Lord and Savior, because many of the people who did profess this acceptance were doing a lot of the bad stuff. I was twelve, but I understood racism, and the Christians who supported it. I understood and even approved of human free will, but I didn't like what God was doing with God's will. I didn't like how things were set up. I blamed God.

And so I stood there and looked at the sky and said this:

"I know you are there. I know you want me, but I refuse you. I want nothing to do with you, or your church. Go away and leave me alone. I will be just fine."

And then I went in and put on my PJ's, asked my mom for milk and cookies, read some Tolkien, and slept peacefully.

I may have been apostate, and courageous enough to tell God, but I wasn't stupid enough to tell my mom. So I started my life of closet apostasy, and ironically, serious hypocrisy. I did decline baptism. I told my parents that I did not feel ready, and that surely they wouldn't want me to be baptized until it felt right. They looked worried, but they agreed.

I eventually taught Sunday school, because it was easier than sitting in Sunday school. I was president of the youth group because somebody had to do it. I went to camp. I sang because it pleased my mother, then I did precisely whatever pleased me the rest of the time. And I counted the days until my escape.

I had some close scrapes running my own life, but I was making it. Sure I was scared, hiding a lot, faking a lot, but it was only temporary.

Mario

My parents settled us into the Chicago suburb of Oak Park. It was still on the EL train line, but the schools were good. With one working-class wage, we were at the low end of the local economic scale. For most of my childhood, my parents slept on a fold-out sofa in the second-floor rented flat we called home. Some of my friends lived in huge houses with help. Protestants were actually a minority, as the Catholic kids and Jewish kids outnumbered us. Being sanctified was not a topic I ever brought up. I was not cool or popular as it was. But I made my way, mostly among the other non-upper echelon kids.

Late in grade school, Mario Spampinato moved into the neighborhood. He was a sweet kid, but bigger than the other boys. He was six feet tall and shaving in the eighth grade. His family was more working class than mine. Somebody said his mom was divorced. That didn't happen much at our school. We walked home together some days. He interested me in ways that I had no language for. And then there was the motorcycle. He was fourteen and he had a bike. This also did not happen at our school. The rest of us had bicycles.

It was a swift little flat bench Honda. More scooter than cruiser, but to my eyes it was Marlon Brando's Triumph. One afternoon, I talked him into showing it off to me. My crush for the bike instantaneously exceeded my crush on the boy. My mother, of course, would have no truck with this boy or his bike. But as far as I knew, Jesus was coming back any day in glory and anger. I was apostate, and facing a difficult time of being left behind for an apocalyptic tribulation followed by an eternity in hell. Seemed like a boy with a fast bike and criminal potential might come in handy.

You hang on tight when you are on the back of a flat bench seat, even if you are just flying up and down the alley. Tight enough to develop what passes for love and lust at fourteen.

I lost track of the boy the next year at high school. The bike stayed in my heart forever. And I knew right there and then that I wanted to grip my own handlebars.

Mercy and Goodness

While in a foxhole in France, just before the mustard gas reached him, my Grandpa Hubbell made a deal with God. "If I live, I will preach." This deal has been offered up a hundred thousand times, I am sure.

Grandpa kept the deal. He came home and married the daughter of an Appalachian hillbilly preacher and spoke the Gospel all over southern Illinois—a place that was not exactly wanting for the Word—between the two wars and after. It didn't pay very well, so he also carried the mail.

I only sat under his preaching on a couple of occasions. He was a gentle exhorter. He spoke much of Love. My mother said he also lived it. Maybe the hellfire preachers made more money.

The only sermon of his that I remember had dogs in it. He was preaching the 23rd Psalm. Mostly there's sheep in that thing, but when he got to the bit about Mercy and Goodness following, he made Mercy and Goodness out to be sheepdogs. He made a good deal out of Mercy and Goodness being hard work, with a lot of running after and nipping at heels. He pointed out that it wasn't Mercy and Punishment. It was redundant goodness, not carrot or stick.

God's answer to rebellion and apostasy is not anger. But God does let the dogs out. Through my adolescence, I felt Mercy and Goodness at my heels. I heard their yips and low growls of warning. I didn't admit to myself that I knew them. But I did.

When I finally reached the velocity necessary to escape my childhood, I thought I had fooled my parents about my whole rebellion deal. Turns out they were pretty clear on the path I was taking. My mother worried a lot. I was the one who was deaf and blind to the truth that their love for me made letting me go a risky business indeed. The two of them prayed for me, as they had every day since they knew I was in the womb.

The night before I left home for good, my dad came into my room and sat next to me on my bed, and handed me a wrapped gift. It was a Bible Book House kind of plaque. It said, "There are only two things a parent can give a child–Roots and Wings." He said to me, "Now's the time for wings, honey–Don't fly too far, ok?"

Surrender

At eighteen, by a narrow margin, I not only achieved the velocity required to get out of my parent's home, but I avoided being sucked into the black hole of the nearby Christian college. I was accepted at a prestigious liberal arts school with no tests, texts, or lectures. It followed Mortimer Adler's regimen of the Great Books. Freshman year, we read Sophocles in Greek. Did science with Archimedes and contemplated Plato and then worked our way through history. Nobody told you what to think, they just asked questions and put up with know-it-all eighteen year olds like me. All this in the lovely city of Santa Fe, New Mexico—1500 miles from home—paid for, of course, by my parents. Ah, Freedom.

I drank beer. I rode horses. I got myself a guy. It was great.

Until sophomore year.

They had three questions at St. John's. It was recommended that you bring them to every text:

What is the author saying?

Is it true?

And if it is true, how does it change your life?

I should have smelled a trap.

Because sophomore year we read the Bible. Stem to stern. And asking the questions were these two guys, our academic midwives and nursemaids. At one end of the seminar table was Michael Ossorgin, conceived in Russia, born in Paris just after the Revolution, graduate of the Sorbonne, Russian Orthodox Bishop. He chain-smoked and drank hard and glowed with holiness. This worried me a bit.

At the other end of the table was Robert Sacks, Jew, slight of frame and fettered by cerebral palsy. He occasionally shouted, often laughed, and was a planetary expert on the Book of Genesis. He scared me a bit. They were absolutely nothing like anything I had ever seen before, only they were like everything I knew was true.

The Old Testament wasn't too bad. All those years of Sunday school helped me sound pretty smart—at least I thought so. Then we read the New Testament—in Greek—slowly. And there was that pesky Jesus, purported God. And those dirty questions. And the holy guys at the ends of the table.

In the beginning was the Word (reason, ratio, relationship, everything that ever made sense) And the Word was God. And this Word lights up everyone who ever came into the world. So often they do not recognize it. But if they do recognize it they become completely alive. (paraphrase of John 1)

What is the author saying? God isn't a keeper of lists and rules. There is no list of sinners and saints. God is Connection. Jesus was the example of that connection. He did not die to protect us from his abusive daddy, He died because we die, and he is connected to us even in that and beyond that. God is already at work in every single human, because it is impossible for God not to be. And realizing this connection exists connects you to everything and that is what it means to be consciously alive.

Is it true? It sounded an echo in my soul, to quote an old song. It rang my bell. It made math and science and language and religion all one subject, a seamless garment.

How did it change my life? I found that the truth wasn't in the book, or in other people—glowing or not—and it wasn't in the discussion or the dogma, or the reading, it was inside me, and I recognized it, and I began to live.

I walked out of the seminar hall into the foothills of the Sangre de Christo Mountains and I looked at the sky and I said:

"I know you are there/here. I know you want me/have me. I surrender."

And nothing changed and everything changed. But a conversation started that night that has never really stopped. I accepted Life on Life's terms. God is God. The deal is what it is. Huge pieces of the deal hurt. A lot of the people are unmitigated screw-ups, including me. But I am awake, alive, connected, real. I fake less. I am scared less.

And I have to surrender every day. It is not a one-time conversion sort of thing. I am asked to accept things as they are, not as I would have them be. It is the hard path to peace. It is the hardest of all the disciplines, and the most important.

Surrender is the only cure for rebellion. Surrender requires repentance. It sounds like quitting and laying down and dying, but it is not.

The paradox is that it is also the open gate to revolution, and subversion. Subversion means to turn over from the bottom; revolution means to turn around an axis; repentance means to change your course 180 degrees. If you combine those three things, you get a three dimensional recipe for catastrophic change. This kind of change would be like old Earth flipping its magnetic poles while reversing its rotation on its axis, and stopping in mid-path to retreat in its orbit. That is the kind of change I am talking about. That is why the prophets of pert near true talk about second births, and resurrection and dying to yourself, and being a new creature.

This is what I learned at St John's: if that riptide tugging at your knees is God, dive for the undertow and drown. It is the only way to become alive.

Wrack and Ruin

I got married on my 20th birthday because it was the only way I could figure to not have to come home for summer vacations from college. I was also crazy in love. My mother told me that I wasn't finished figuring out who I was, and so I shouldn't pick someone permanent. What I couldn't tell my mother was that I had recently cancelled my apostasy, and so I was pretty sure that everything was going to be great from here on out. I did arrange to be baptized by some Quonset-hut Santa Fe Episcopalians and invited my parents, which surprised them mightily.

I spent my twenties baking bread, quilting, canning, sewing baby clothes and re-embracing a slightly kinder and gentler version of my parents' religion. We moved to Oregon, and I found the Quakers, a religion that seemed to offer enough room to breathe.

The Quakers had allowed women preachers for the last 300 years. I met a couple of them. Laura Cammack Trachsel, who spotted me at a gathering of Evangelical church ladies and quietly asked me if I wanted to come and talk with her about deeper spirituality. She was a woman who had gone to China in the 1920's and came screaming out of there with Mao on her trail. Mao kept her husband Jack for a couple of years. She made it out with three babies and came home to be a pastor of a church when women just weren't doing that much. Laura introduced me to Vivian Thornburg, a local Quaker pastor who has the most amazing, no-nonsense ability to love fully without being smarmy about it. She saw what I was capable of and expected me to do it.

This was convenient, because weirdly, my mother's genetic plan for me was mutating into something else. I was no kind of preacher's wife. But I started to preach. The sermons came to me as my babies came, surprises—every one. I didn't volunteer to preach, I gestated messages and then at some point they just had to come out. The Quakers seemed to think this was just as natural as the babies, and that kinda freaked me out.

When my Grandpa, now near ninety, found out I was preaching, he had my Aunt Geneva send me his pulpit Bible. He sent me a letter telling me that he wouldn't be needing it where he was headed, but he was proud I would carry on the Gospel tradition.

Then my mother died. She was only 61. I was only 31. We had just started to like each other again. The two grandchildren helped with that. Then she got the cancer that had stolen her own mother, and she was gone. And something in me broke. Wide open.

I had rebelled against what she wanted me to be, and then tried to be that thing. Neither had really worked. I was ready to admit that. So I made some space to find out what I wanted to be. Mother, sure. Wife—part of the deal. Daughter, more full-time now, as my dad was withering without Mom and I talked him into moving out West and into our home. Preacher, a weird hobby, but it was feeding something in me and in the world. All these things were important, but I felt like I was rolled up in cotton batting. Some piece of me was yelling to be let out of the basement.

Losing a good mother is like surviving a tornado. You crawl into the cellar to survive it, and then the storm just rips the house off above your head. All the history, all the expectations for the future, the carefully constructed walls and spaces, the emotional tea towels and photos are just gone, and you start all over. Some people gather the pieces and rebuild the same house. Some people start on their own dream. Some people just move away. I came up and stood there in the emotional wrack and ruin, nothing between me and the world. And I had this thought:

"I could get a motorcycle—she's not here—she can't stop me."

It was the only good thing I could think of to do.

Rebel

I started serious plotting to get two wheels in 1993. Mom was gone, Dad was in my house, the girls were twelve and seven, we had a dog and two cats and I had decided to go back to school. Life was getting pretty dang serious. And my desire for a bike grew, unabated.

When I first started to talk about it at the dinner table, no one believed I was serious. My dad's remark was, "Be sure to get a helmet." The girls rolled their eyes. The husband looked up at me, concerned, but then went back to his dinner.

I took the general non-objection as a blessing. I walked into a few dealerships, but it was clear that there was no way for me to finance something new. I talked to my friend Owen, who was the only person I knew at the time who owned a bike. I talked him into taking me for a ride on his Honda Shadow. My second Honda ride. It was pretty great, except for the part about sitting on the back seat.

Then one early summer evening, I was sitting on Owen's porch. A rider came up the street on a pretty, blue, 250 cc Honda Rebel. Owen said, "That is exactly the bike you ought to start with." I allowed as how he was exactly right. The rider got to the end of the street and turned around. Coming back slowly, it was clear that the rider was female. She slowed some more as she approached us. Then she stopped. She called up to the house.

"The mechanic at the dealership told me that there was someone on this block who is looking to buy a bike—don't suppose you would know who?"

"This woman here!" said Owen.

I was already walking towards the bike. "She's a beaut! What are you asking for her?"

"A thousand."

"Would you take payments?"

"No, I need the cash."

"Would you take eight hundred cash right now?" asked Owen from the porch.

"Owen!–I don't have it!"

"I'll go get my checkbook. You can make payments to me."

And that is how I came to own a motorcycle. Owen had to ride her to my garage for me. I had no skills and no endorsement on my license. The husband and the father were surprised, but they couldn't say they hadn't been warned.

Failure

Owen taught me how to ride, first on the back of his, then with careful explanations and experiments at the local high school parking lot. My biggest problem was shifting. I was shifting at random moments when I thought I ought to shift. I was missing a lot. I tried shifting by looking at the tachometer. But then I ran into things. I tried shifting by the sound of the engine, still not good. Then Owen had the epiphany. "Peg—you are sitting on a 250 cubic centimeter vibrator—when it feels good—SHIFT." *Et Voila.*

I took the new Rebel to the Department of Motor Vehicles. As a permitted learner, but not a licensed rider, I had arrived accompanied by an experienced rider. Just like with cars, you can practice riding on the streets with an experienced friend. Unlike practice driving in a car, if you make a big mistake, all your friend on the other bike can do is scream, and then call 911. That day, he stood on the sidelines and watched as I went through my paces on my shiny new friend. At a mere 300lbs she was just the light, nimble bike that you wanted for the test.

They do this test off-road, in a parking lot that is painted with a test course. The tester that day was a serious-looking young man with a clipboard. He inspected my bike and my gear and gave me instructions and then the go-ahead. I did great at the slalom cones. I braked from speed without skidding. I demonstrated the ability to use turn signals and the horn without problem. I downshifted on a corner. I passed all his tasks with ease until the last one. This was the "tight turn trick."

Painted on the pavement was a three-sided bay that was precisely the size of two parking spaces. You were required to enter on the left side going at least 15 mph, and then to execute a turn inside this bay and exit on the right side without touching the white lines. There was a dot painted at the apex for reference.

I had practiced a U-turn on a two-lane road, but this was considerably tighter. I gave it my best shot. Gas to 15. Entered bay. Braked. Turned at apex. Made a critical mistake. I looked down at the dot on the pavement, and then the bike was down, and I was standing over her. I looked up. Owen had his eyes covered, cringing. The clipboard guy was shaking his head and walking towards me.

I was furious and humiliated.

I don't remember picking up my bike. I do remember putting the front wheel back down on the ground from somewhere in midair. Apparently, I was pumping a bit of adrenaline. I remember the front tire bouncing as I set it back down. I looked up again at the clipboard guy. He stopped, took one step backward and made a "settle down" gesture with his free hand, eyes wide open.

"Ma'am, you ok?"

"Grrr—I flunked—right?"

"You are going to have to wait three days to take the test again—but you can take it again—I am sure you will pass next time—ma'am."

"Grrr."

Guy to Owen: "Make sure she takes a few minutes to calm down before you guys ride home, ok?"

I did calm down a bit. The fury wore off with the stress hormones. But I was in complete freak-out about flunking. I just could not believe it. I called another sympathetic friend.

"I flunked! I can't believe it. I flunked!"

"Peggy, chill, it's just like flunking a quiz at school, only with infinite do-overs."

"Excuse ME! I have NEVER flunked a quiz."

"Never? Never in 20 years of school?"

"Of course not!"

"Um, Okay—it's like getting fired from a job—you get another job."

"Oh, give me a break—NO ONE has ever fired ME."

"Man... then it is like getting dumped."

"What!? Dumped? I don't think so!"

"You know what, Peggy? You needed this—God decided it was your turn."

My friend was right. I was in a failure deficit situation, and that is not good. I was 35 years old and I had never learned the Spiritual Discipline of Failure. This is not an optional discipline. And as it turned out in the next decade of my life, I was going to be in a couple of big situations where success by any normal standard of success was not going to be possible, and God needed me to be fit for the task. So, I started a series of practicums in the art of not getting it anything close to right.

It's a tough class.

The core truth of this discipline is that you must learn to take your focus off of outcome and put it onto process. I had been hung up on flunking and not looking at how I flunked. That is a killer of a mistake. It not only can get you actually killed in certain situations, it kills learning and joy the rest of the time. It drastically increases fear, because there is always a dreaded outcome, and never a preventative within your control. I needed to forget about the test, and learn the crucial lesson that motorcycles will go wherever you put your eyes. In a tight turn you look out to your exit, not down at the pavement. When you learn this lesson, tight turns cease to be scary. This is good, because Life offers many opportunities for the quick U-turn.

I don't really see God as some sort of cosmic tester with a clipboard, but I have learned to leave the outcomes up to God. When faced with an experience that looks like failure, I take a deep breath, calm down, and look at what I was doing. Inevitably, there was a part of the situation that I was trying to control that was really not in my power, and part of the situation that actually was in my control that I was ignoring, or didn't recognize. Then I let go of the former and focus on the latter and sign up for do-overs.

Fortunately for me, I worship a God of infinite do-overs.

The next weekend, my elderly father went out into our street with a can of spray paint and a tape measure and made me a copy of the DMV test. He bought me a few cones at the hardware store. I practiced.

I also took a motorcycle riding and safety class. The next time I took the test, as I came out of that tight corner, I was looking up. Just in time to see Owen perched off to the side on a berm doing the white crane pose like the Karate Kid.

Rocinante

I spent the next winter paying off Owen. I also finished a degree in professional counseling with a minor in pastoral ministry. I got a job as a pastoral counselor. I worked with people recovering from trauma. I took a few pastoral gigs here and there.

I rode the little Reb in all kinds of weather. Fresh love is frequent and enthusiastic. Out here in Oregon, we don't get much snow or ice, so you can ride 12 months a year if you are willing to be wet and cold. I started saving for a good set of leathers.

By early summer of '94, I had come to a conclusion. Two hundred and fifty cc's was not going to be enough. She was just fine on two-lane back roads, but when I took her out on the interstate, things got sketchy. She had enough engine to do the speed limit, but she was wound out–full tilt–at 70. Acceleration is one of the things that bikes do better than cars, so you need to keep that card up your sleeve. We also got pushed around by truck wakes. You feel these in a car; the 18-wheelers kick up turbulence beside and behind. A bike is assaulted by this wash. The Rebel often got pushed into the next lane, which wasn't okay when that lane was occupied.

It felt like cheating, but I started looking. That is when I met Rocinante, in the back barn at Taylor Honda/Kawasaki in Woodburn, Oregon. She was the last year's model with no miles–left behind. I have always had sympathy for the left behind. She was silver and midnight blue. The height of her seat was a precise fit for the inseam of my jeans. At 500 lbs., she had 750 cc's–lots of power–nobody's pushover. I walked away once and thought about it, and then the next weekend, I rode up and asked to test ride her. When I got off the Reb, I said goodbye, because I knew what was going to happen. I had carried the little bike's title with me.

I cranked the Kaw up and eased in the clutch and pulled on the throttle and nearly blew myself off the back. My left hand had to lunge for the bar. Three times around the lot then out on the main road for a bit and then I came back in and parked up front and walked in and made the best deal a smitten woman could make with old man Taylor. He kept the Reb.

Kawasaki calls her a Vulcan after the God of Fire, volcanoes and metalworking. I named her Rocinante after Don Quixote's steed.

Three days later, in Newberg, Oregon, I was recorded as a Minister of the Gospel by the Quakers. We don't ordain or make ministers. We think God does that. We just try to pay attention and notice what God is doing. That bunch of Quakers seemed to think that God was doing something with me. I did not argue. I did ride the new bike to Newberg that week.

Part 2:
Shiny Side Up, Rubber Side Down

There is a learning curve to being an epic protagonist. And by curve, I mean climbing straight up a tall building spidey-wise. Budding young heroes rarely enjoy much of it in the moment. It really only gets good when you are old and telling the tale at the VFW hall. But the important thing is never to be afraid

to be the hero of your own story.

No one else is going to do it.

How I got to Scotts Mills

I took the blessed notice of my faith community and went to work; part-time associate pastor and part-time trauma healer. Sadly, my young ministry didn't survive its first major test. That test involved, amongst other things, being the target of sexual harassment, conflict about how to deal with that, and deep disappointment when the powers that be protected the harasser and not me. I tried using my freshly minted Christian Counseling degree to work things out in something like a healthy manner. I failed. When the harasser started threatening one of my children, I ran. The Quaker Elders told me to keep my mouth shut. The people I was working with, my co-pastors and appointed mentors, felt free to open theirs. When word started to get out, so did some very ugly slander about me. I had a lawyer craft one of those "Stop it—I mean it" letters. Taking an assertive step to protect myself did not help my standing.

I weathered the couple of months of depression that followed, but as I came out of it I was pretty clear about the fact that I was done with pastoral ministry and likely done with Quakers. But I just couldn't quit God. Apostasy Round Two wasn't a real possibility; all I could muster was some feeble fist shaking. I knew it wasn't God I was mad at. I figured I would just stay away from churches.

One warm morning that summer, I had the luxury of an empty house. I was steeping myself in quiet contemplation when someone said in a clear and calm voice, "Go check on my people in Scotts Mills." I looked up. I thought my father had come back inside. I called out and then walked about. I was alone. I was also seriously spooked. The voice had been perfectly external. It did not repeat itself or elaborate. I tried to shake it off. It stuck like stink, and it reeked of God.

I examined the instruction. I knew there was a town in the valley called Scotts Mills. I had ridden the bike through it a couple of times. Picturesque little hamlet in the foothills of the Cascade Mountains, out past Silverton. I knew there was a Friends Church there, but I had never been in it—a little gingerbread Victorian steeple house that would have been frowned upon as too ornate by good Kansas Quakers.

Sunday morning came around and I tried to pretend that I had forgotten, but I had not. It was not the sort of voice you could forget. I told the family that I was going out. Eyebrows elevated, but I joined the club of non-elaborators. I found the town and found the church just as the bell chimed in the righteous. It was a pretty little room. They had apparently remained too poor to wreck their building with anything modern. The service was led by an elderly fellow who knew his Bible, and asked of it no nuanced questions. There were about 25 worshippers, and no chance of sneaking in and out unobserved.

At the rise of the meeting, I was greeted by all. Most of them seemed to be named Magee. I met a 95-year stalwart named Edith, who introduced me to her daughter-in-law Margaret, and her daughter Laura, and Laura's three daughters. Sarah was five, about to start kindergarten and had new crayons. Rachel was three and was too busy playing with a stained-glass rainbow to bother with me. April Hope was just six months. She smiled at me, so I snuck in a cuddle. Then I got out of there.

"Hey—Yahweh the Great and Powerful! Your people in Scotts Mills seem just fine to me—as if you needed me to tell you that." Really, the whole thing had not seemed worthy of a Voice. And I had no intention of going back.

Then mid-week, the phone rang. It was the clerk of the meeting at Scotts Mills. She told me that she had found out that I was a recorded minister and wondered if I was free on Sundays—the retired interim pastor needed to go to Idaho for six weeks. I sighed tremendously and rolled my eyes heavenward. See, I was wise to this Divine plotter and I knew that this God was quite the DIY rehabber. I instantly spotted the sneak intervention that would get me back in a church. I was not feeling cooperative. So I quickly thought of the most passive aggressive way possible to get out of this.

"Well," I said, "Your information is correct and I am not engaged on Sundays at this point, but my availability is really very limited. I can't make it out for Sunday School, or Bible study, or prayer meeting. I do not have time for visiting the sick or the homebound. About all I could do would be walk in at the last minute on Sundays, preach a sermon, and leave. I am sure that you need more than that." "Nope" she said, "We can do all the rest of that stuff, all we need is pulpit supply. Can you start the week after next?"

Passive aggression had worked about as well as it usually does. I had no good excuse left. I heard myself agree. I was irritated and mystified—that always produces good sermon material.

The following Monday, the phone rang again at my house. The pastor of Silverton Friends Church was on the phone. "Peggy, I'm out at Silverton Hospital, I hear they have left you in charge of Scotts Mills..." "Oh, no," I said "Sunday only, nothing extra, blah blah, backpeddle, blah, evade blah, ..." And being the kind gentle Christian that he was, he said, "Peggy, shut up for a minute! Margaret Magee is here, she's been injured. Shot. Laura is dead, the little girls are dead. Laura's husband is in custody."

Things I didn't know: Laura was getting a divorce. From an abusive husband. Who came down from Seattle. Despite the restraining order. And blew them away.

I forgot all my self-indulgent bullshit, and dove in.

Here's what I want you to know about how I got to Scotts Mills: I hate it. To this day I hate it. If God can look at the playing field and move a trauma healer here or there because they are going to be needed, well then God can jolly well send a voice to Laura Magee, or her mother, or her grandmother, and calmly instruct one of those perfectly-willing-to-listen Christian women to get those babies the heck out of town! I believe they would have done it. And lived.

Scotts Mills Friends Church suffered, and they grieved, and they clawed their way back up, and chose to go on believing, and turned outward and started a ministry to prevent family violence, and opened a women's shelter. They grew and thrive today.

Blast it all, Scotts Mills was also the rehab of one bad-attitude female preacher. And I kinda hate that too. I would trade my rehab for the life of that smiling babe. In a nano-second. And it might be wrong. Maybe I would have never gone to Africa, or started a new Quaker thing, or written this or any other book. Other people might be dead. But I would probably do it—the trade. But I don't get that choice. I also don't get the choice to deny that I heard that voice. Because I did. My only choice was, and is, to obey or not.

Running

I was in need of healing, though I didn't really think of it that way at the time. I drained myself dry in those first few weeks in Scotts Mills. Trying to be a bit of Providence to a heartbroken community takes a lot of energy and I really hadn't possessed much when I started. What I had or didn't have did not matter a whole lot. I understood that I was needed. When the old preacher got back from Idaho, they asked me to stay on. I agreed.

I had previously scheduled a personal retreat for just a few weeks later and I knew that I needed to take it, despite the circumstances. I told them that I needed one weekend and they graciously told me to take it. I had 96 hours set aside for a ride: Friday noon until Tuesday noon.

I left Salem, Oregon, just after one in the afternoon. The official plan was to go over to the coast and go a little ways south if weather permitted, or stay at a town named Florence if it rained. It was October, so rain was likely. The weather did not look good at the start. My 'Retreat Rule' was no TV, no newspapers, the Bible, and no biker bars.

I talk to God on these trips, even when I am not particularly happy with God. I initiated the conversation with the very simple request of a little sunshine. It appeared, a small patch of blue always before me, but never over me, and I chased it all the way to the coast. Refueling at Florence, God spoke to me in the more mundane voice of a gas-station attendant, who said, "You know, you can go a long ways with a little bit of blue sky."

This had been the condition of my soul all year: rained on and chasing but never catching the bit of blue ahead of me. I turned south on Highway 101 and rode faster. I realized that I was running when I hit the California border before dark, three hundred miles from home. I'm not sure what I was running to, or running from, but I was definitely running. I slept with the sound of the ocean in my ears and these words in my head:

"Wherever you run, I AM with you."

I spent Saturday buzzing through the redwoods and down Highway One—an even smaller road and closer to the Pacific Ocean. A guardian angel on a BMW bike pulled me over to warn me of an oil spill on the road ahead that surely would have taken me down, and I had lunch with two very old gay men on a Harley and a Motto Guzzi who wanted me to go with them to Baja. It was tempting, but my conversation with them caused me to explain to them and to myself why my commitments back in Oregon really did matter to me.

Later, God and I had a nice light conversation about God's favorite color, and I was forced to take a very tiring detour over a mountain. I ended a ten-hour riding day in Bodega Bay, talking to a prophetic waiter. I had gotten a notion in my head about visiting a certain church I had once heard about, and asked the waiter for directions. He was surprised at the street names I gave him and asked why I wanted to go into that part of the Tenderloin district of San Francisco. I said I was going to church and he said, "Ah, you are going to Glide Church. You are going to be OK."

Sunday morning, I got up early and made the Golden Gate Bridge by 9 a.m. I made the 10 a.m. service at Glide United Methodist Church. I had heard a rumor about this place, but I was in no way prepared for what I found. It was surreal. On my left was a prostitute who told me that she always, "Stays up for church—it's the only thing that gets me through." On my right was a guy in drag, I think, and the people in the pew in front of me were from France. They let the house band loose, and the stained glass shook.

I am normally a strong introvert who dislikes and distrusts "enthusiasm" in worship. But that morning I bumped into the very real presence of a Holy, Righteous, and Rockin' God, and I clapped, and I danced, and I sang, and I cried, and somewhere during a song called "Restore my Joy," it was. I was healed; I carried no more wounds. My biochemistry was the same, my emotions were the same, but I was whole rather than damaged. I don't have any other words for it.

After the service, the prostitute said to me, "You came a long way to get this, didn't you?" I said, "About 700 miles." She laughed and said, "Looks like longer than that, but it was worth it, wasn't it?" It was.

The ride home was a lark, and I played a familiar game with my cosmic travel agent. Here is a true thing—if you play with God, God plays right back. Sometimes on the road I play a challenge game where I name what conditions I wish to sleep under and see if God can produce them. It's a silly game, but it is fun. That afternoon, I requested a place to sleep in the trees with some Mexican food—a modest request. Within an hour I was registered in a little motel and restaurant on a wooded hill run by a very nice Mexican family. The only drawback was when I discovered that the room next to mine was "Sealed by the order of the Coroner." It seems someone had "checked out" rather permanently the night before. I stayed, and in a perusal of scripture that night, I found this:

Esther 4:16, "Pray for me, and if I perish, I perish."

I have always liked Esther. She was level headed and used what she had. She had real chutzpah. I found in her request a guide for spiritual adventurers. Ask for help, then accept what you get.

Many miles north the next day, my joy still intact, I knew I would only make it to Grants Pass, a small redneck kind of town in Southern Oregon. So I made my request as ridiculous as I could. I wanted to sleep by a river, find a one-hour photo shop that was open after eight, and have New York cheesecake and cognac for a bedtime snack. At nine, photos in hand, cheesecake and cognac on a patio next to the river, I was left to wonder at the theologically ludicrous notion that the Creator of the Universe was spoiling me in a rather personal manner.

Tuesday noon, I walked into my home and met my husband, who asked if I had a good time. I acknowledged I had. He asked if I had gotten farther than Florence, and I handed him my pictures.

"Peggy, that's the Golden Gate Bridge."

"Yes dear."

"Peggy, that's you."

"Yes, it is."

"Peggy, that's in California!"

"Yes, it did seem a little weird; very much like California."

"Peggy, what were you doing in San Francisco?"

"Getting healed, I think, yes, getting healed."

Quakers

Sometimes I call Rosie "The Holy Kaw." This is because I never seem to be able to take her out on the road without having conversations about God and Faith. Maybe it is our charism. When we are out on the road, my mode of transport is obvious, even when she is parked outside, because I am always wearing leathers and there is a full-face helmet on the counter next to me. I usually take a seat at the counter because the leathers don't bend so good, and it's a pain to get in and out of them.

I always mind my own business, but that never seems to prevent other people from minding my business with me. A big trucker plants himself next to me. The correlation between truckers and bikers is significantly high.

"Hey, pretty lady, where you riding to today?"

They never seem to be able to leave the solo female biker thing alone. But I take no offense. I give a brief itinerary. Weather is discussed—I never discount weather info from a trucker.

"So, whatcha do when you aren't ridin?"

"I'm a Quaker preacher."

This always stops them for a moment. Silence ensues, which is appropriate since Quakers often worship in silence. We think people talk too much and listen not enough. We try and let God get in the edgewise word.

The next question is often, "I thought you guys were all dead."

We are frequently confused with the Shakers—an 18th century sect that did not believe in procreation and hence mostly died out. Quakers have been around since 1652, have had women preachers all that time, and, for good or ill, we do have children.

"Nope, we're still going strong."

"And you ride motorcycles?"

Confusion with the Amish is next. Quakers have no conscience against technology.

"Yep, and cars and airplanes and everything."

"Hunh." I can see the confusion generalizing. I decide to volunteer a bit of information.

"And, we don't look like the Quaker Oats guy anymore."

"I can see that—but you are eating the oatmeal."

"Oh yes, we are very religious about the oatmeal."

Actually, Quakers have never produced, sold, or had any official connection with commercial oatmeal production. Those guys are trading off our good name. I think we should get a discount, but we don't. Sometimes I just can't resist messing with the heads of random truckers.

"So what are y'all about?"

"Oh, you know, the standard Jesus stuff—being good to folks even when they aren't good to you, taking care of the poor, keeping it simple, telling it like it is, not letting anything get between you and God."

"Hunh."

"OK, we don't really care so much about the oatmeal. Cream of Wheat is perfectly acceptable." (Got caught by my own preaching once again.)

"You know, I always thought Jesus would make a good biker."

"Me too, buddy, me too."

Subversive

Along with the trucker/Quaker conversation there are some other conversations that I have that are so typical that I can see them coming. One of my favorites typically involves the curiosity of a small child. It goes like this:

I am sliding into a freeway rest stop in high summer—families out touring en masse. When I first dismount, I am completely encased in a leather and Kevlar exoskeleton, including a full-face helmet. It is not obvious who, or even what, I am. So when I whip the lid off, folks are often surprised to see a woman emerging from this cocoon. It's a little like sipping your Coke and finding out that it's a root beer. I disconcert expectations. After the startle, some people are interested. Little girls are curious, especially when they are in that sweet spot of curiosity and boldness of early grade school. Their dads and brothers usually compliment me on the machine—girls want to know all about me.

"Are you a lady?" (By which she means gender female?)

"Yes, indeed!"

"Do you have a daddy?" (Are you married?)

"Yes—I am married."

"He lets you ride a motorcycle?"

And then I lean down close, look the little girl right in the eyes, and whisper to her soul,

"I didn't ask—You don't have to ask!"

Subversion is one of the basic Jesus things. The first shall be last, the up shall be down, etc. The kingdom of Heaven is right here among us and it does not follow the rules of this world. Some of Jesus' best subversions are not really appreciated well enough. Some of the most intentional had to do with the place of women.

When he let the woman that everyone looked down on pour perfume on his feet, he was subverting the paradigm that said that righteous men do not let any woman but their wife touch them. When he let Martha's sister Mary study at his feet he was admitting her to the Yeshiva—she was a coed in the class of men. When He appears first to Magdalene on Easter morning and sends her to tell the disciples he is subverting the paradigm that said that the testimony of women did not count.

Just being out solo on the bike, I am subverting the same nasty, rotten, old paradigms. When I speak to little girls about their freedom, I get into the same danger zone He did. Some people don't like it. But the little girls know they are seeing something new.

Their moms ask similar questions, usually in the privacy of the ladies room, and they ask more obliquely.

"Does your husband ride with you?"

My answers to the mothers are also a little more oblique. I used to tell them that my husband didn't care for motorcycles, but that we have an agreement that allows me all the safe fun I can handle. I left alone the issue of what constitutes safe fun and who decides how much I can handle.

The mothers exhibit extreme surprise when I am off on a multi-state, multi-day ride. It is amazing to me how many adult women have never traveled farther than the mall unaccompanied by someone. They will travel in groups and gaggles, but rarely solo. Sometimes they get far enough into the questioning to ask where I am headed to that night. I often answer that I do not know, that I will stop when and wherever I get tired. I choose to trust God to supply the place. They usually stop asking questions at this point and back away. I become alien and a wee bit scary.

A Baptist minister once asked me how long Quakers had allowed women in the ministry. I answered, "Oh, 350 years or so—from the get-go."

And we didn't ask—because you don't have to ask.

Weather

Living one day at a time, Enjoying one moment at a time, accepting hardship as the pathway to peace. Taking as He did, this sinful world as it is, not as I would have it.

-Reinhold Niebuhr

Unmediated travel requires you to accept the weather. You can accept it and stay in the barn, or you can accept it and ride in it.

The ambient temp on a bike is almost never just right. You are usually a little too warm or a little bit cold. Sometimes a lot. There is a fancy formula for calculating wind chill, but faster equals colder every time. On the bike you create your own wind. If it is 50 degrees outside and you are going 65 mph, the perceived temp is 39. If you are wet, it's worse. And that is just the wind you are creating.

The regular old wind does not want you to forget it, so it pushes you around. If it is steady and from the side, you crib into it like an airplane does to correct and stay on a straight path. But then the tricky old wind will just intermittently hold its breath for a couple of seconds like an angry two year old, and you start flying off to the side. Steady headwinds are okay; they just suck up your gas mileage. A tailwind is always your friend. Variable side gusts, like you get on the Oregon coast, are my least favorite. It is like having an invisible tormentor who follows you all day, frequently but randomly hitting you with a heavy sofa cushion. Fighting such a wind decreases my stamina by at least 30%.

You can ride in cold and dry. You hear about people up North who put on chains or studded tires and ride in the snow—riders gotta do what riders gotta do. I own heated gloves that plug into the battery of the bike. I tend to lose feeling in my fingers while riding, a combination of cold and vibration. There is a term for this; around here it is called Oregon White Finger, named that by loggers. When this happens, your fingers lose blood flow and turn white; sensation goes right after. I have a personal rule that when I lose feeling in the third finger of the same hand, I have to get in and get warm. I find that holding a cup of hot coffee is painful but brings the blood flow back. I ride less in the cold than when I first fell in love with riding. Old love is still good love.

Wet and cold is very dangerous. Once, on a cold rainy ride through the forests of Northern California, I managed to pull into home of a couple of Quaker high elves, just as my personal resources of heat and hope were depleted. They fed me and sheltered me. When the next morning looked worse, weather-wise, Galadriel herself gifted me with a heated vest from her own closet that might have saved my life that day.

Heat stroke and dehydration can be just as dangerous as cold and wet. The opposite of wind chill is called desiccation. Not good. I am a fan of my skin, and wear my leathers in almost every weather condition. If it is hot, I may not wear much underneath—I have ridden long days in nothing that did not come from Langlitz Leathers or Victoria's Secret, all black, of course. I also have a lighter-armored summer jacket.

All of this takes away from the unmediated piece, and the acceptance piece. What you really do is accommodate the weather, except when you have to occasionally surrender and just get out of it. Learning when to accept, when to accommodate and when to surrender is wisdom that only comes with seat-time. I would also point out to Brother Niebuhr that Jesus didn't always accept the world the way it was. He occasionally commanded it into peaceful stillness.

Crooked

"The voice of him who crieth in the wilderness, make straight in the desert a highway for our God. Every Valley shall be exalted, and every mountain and hill shall be made low: and the crooked shall be made straight and the rough places plain."

-Isaiah 40:23-40

One of my favorite roads in America runs between Highway 101 and Highway 1 in far northern California. It is a cold, rainforested, roller coaster of a road. Biker bliss.

I am not going to name the road because too many of you and your Winnebagos already know where it is. But it goes from the redwoods to the ocean, and it just might be the crookedest road on the West Coast. When they made this road through the prehistoric ferniness, they banked those kinks and turns so precisely that a bike can whiz through there at speeds that cars can only dream of. Motorcycles chuckle at the suggested speed limits for those turns.

"Poor cagers–better slow down–Bye-Bye!"

Because of the superb banking, centripetal forces glue the blessedly two-wheeled to the curves, allowing you to lean at angles that just shouldn't work. What appears to you citizens as a slow two-lane road is a four lane white-water rapid to us, and we use all those lanes. If you can see through the next curve, the whole curve is yours to slice. We do make the crooked straight.

We also like the rough places to be plain. Gravel is not your friend on that road. You are balancing on about eight square inches of rubber, four up front and four behind. You need all the contact you can get.

I cannot ride that road without singing Handel's *Messiah* in the fabulous acoustics of my full-face helmet. Specifically, the part where the prophet and lyricist Isaiah shouts out, "Prepare a highway for our God."

Now it might seem at first listen that he is talking about the interstate through Nevada—flat, straight, smooth. But that is because you don't understand. God is the ultimate crotch rocket and humanity is stuck in the Winnebago. God is infinitely nimble, infinitely powerful, God has more lanes than you, and God plays by completely different rules. And God will pass your 'bago on the right or the left like it was a concrete statue. And doesn't that just frost your cake? God so often behaves like a hooligan. Your messiest, most dangerous, serious switchback of a situation is God's pipeline: arrow-straight, smooth and a kick in the pants.

And thus ends the metaphor, because God does not wipe out.

The important thing to do in preparing the road for God, is to get out of God's way. Here is the message of Isaiah, of angels hanging over the heads of shepherds, of John the Baptist: Something big is about to come this way! Clear the runway, turn on the lights, God is about to land a 747 in the middle of a hurricane! You are so going to wet your britches, but seriously, Fear Not!

Talking

> **How come when we talk to God it's called prayer, and when God talks to us it's called Schizophrenia?**
>
> **-Lily Tomlin**

Yes, I talk to God, and angels, and dead people. And yes, I am a mental health professional and a lover of science. And no, I don't think that is a conflict, I just vaguely refer to quantum physics. Quantum physics covers a multitude of weirdnesses.

I once was visiting a good friend in the psych ward. If you have never been in the psych ward, even to visit, your life could be enriched a bit. My friend wanted out–bad. She was a bit pissed that I got to leave and she didn't. We were sitting with the head doc and she ratted me out.

"Peggy gets to leave and she is more delusional than I am!"

The doc chuckles. "No one said you were delusional–just suicidal."

"Peggy thinks God talks to her through her iPod."

The doc laughs and they both look at me. "Right, Peggy?"

Quaker ministers are supposed to be professionally truthful. The doc was looking at me intently now.

"Well, not all the time. Just sometimes. Always good stuff! Encouragement. Very life affirming." I squirmed. My friend was laughing.

"Sorry, we still have to let Peggy leave–I don't think insurance covers what she has."

I think the Divine has infinite ways to reach each of us, including iPod. I do not think one method of reception is more meritorious than any other. I think the universe is awash in God messages. I think God talking is about as common as dirt. In fact, dirt can communicate God, because nature and its processes are some of the best places to look for God.

God talks to me through random strangers all the time. Some of those strangers may even have a little schizophrenia on board—can't stop God. A street fellow stopped me one day and said, "Excuse me, ma'am, but I really have to say, your shadow is looking quite lovely today." Now there are two ways to take that. Random annoying crazy, or a man who was sees things a little differently than the rest of us and chose to speak to the positive that he saw. I take it the second way. And I think that choosing to speak to the positive is always a God thing.

Some people get the inside voice, some don't. Some read God's voice. Some feel God only in the Love of other humans. Some find God in a microscope or a telescope. Some find God in a community; some go to the desert to be alone with God. For some, God is a cosmic force that permeates but does not change or intervene in the world. God can be in the music, or the painting, or in the garden. I believe all these things. For me, the question isn't, "Where is God found?" but, "Where is God *not* found?" The answer is nowhere.

When I am out on the road, I am more open to that of God. I believe God is present in precisely the same density during my busy work days and mundane tasks. But I am often not as present to God. I let things muffle and mediate the space where God is in me. I work on changing that, but I still forget. But out on the road, I cannot forget. The road is real and immediate. So I talk to God, most commonly calling him Jesus. Occasionally I talk to His mother. We talk and we play and random strangers preach the gospel, and saints and angels tag along for the fun of it. If you want to think that I have imaginary friends, I don't care. And if this is mental illness, then I am grateful for it, and glad that insurance won't pay to cure me.

Traction

There is a work of man they call the Bridge of the Gods. Spanning the mighty Columbia River, a short ride east of Portland, Oregon, this bridge connects the states of Oregon and Washington at the approximate site where geologists and Native Americans agree there once was a stone land bridge that eventually fell into to the river. The ancient spirits who guarded that bridge might just still be around.

It is a high bridge. The kind that requires faith because as you go up, you cannot see down on the other side—you feel like you are driving up and into space. I was prepared for that, but I had never motorcycled this route before, so the sign stating that the bridge had a metal grate deck was a surprise to me, and the sign was not visible until it was too late to make any other choice but to cross.

Here is the problem with motorcycles and metal grating. The bike has about four square inches of each tire that contact the road at any time. That is eight square inches of grip altogether. Metal grating reduces those eight inches to a few tiny strips of metal. It is not enough grip. All traction is lost. It is like riding on ice. If all other things are equal and the grating is limited, then inertia is your friend—and if you just hang on, relax and trust, the bike will continue forward without much deviation until you get solid pavement back. You do not dare steer, brake or accelerate. Brother Newton again.

All things were not equal on the Bridge of the Pissed-Off Gods that day. I was traveling north to south and the winds coming up the Columbia Gorge from the west were about 30 miles per hour steady, with gusts exceeding that by a good bit. Without traction, the winds were steadily pushing me to the left, towards the oncoming traffic. I had just enough warning to enter the grated section at the far right edge of a bridge that is 35 feet wide—17.5 feet for me, 17.5 feet for the other guys. At that point, it was a Hail Mary situation. Would my speed get me across the grate before the wind pushed me into the path of a semi?

That was when I made the mistake of looking down, past my feet, through the grate, and hundreds of feet down to the water. My head started to swim and I snapped my eyes back up to the road. An oncoming Winnebago was laying on its horn. As my tire touched the center line, the grate ended and I had enough traction to correct my course. I coasted down to the tollbooth at the foot of this deathtrap. I was shaking badly enough as I tried to fumble into the pockets of my leathers that the toll taker shook her head and waved me on. I had the feeling she had seen rattled bikers before.

Spiritual lives can also lose traction. We can lose our connection with the ground. We can get all slip-slidey. Think about the places where the rubber meets the road in your life. They are not usually the most pleasant places. Friction is implied in traction. But those are the places that keep you grounded, that give you the option of relative control.

I find that if I surround myself only with people who agree with me, that I start to lose my moorings. I get lazy. On the contrary, I feel my connection to God in a very real way when I am around people who don't share my experience of God. They make me think. They make me check my bearings. This is spiritual traction.

I need a regular connection with people honest enough to let me know when my spiritual slip is showing or I have spinach in my teeth. We have all seen the hard public lessons of those who surround themselves with sycophants. Honest friends supply traction.

I lose spiritual traction when I get disconnected from the real, physical needs of the least among us. I have learned that I cannot fix all the problems that I see. But I can do something, every day, every week, every month, to address those problems. Real, fulfilling work increases traction.

All of these conditions describe places where the road can fall below the minimum required grippiness. Sometimes the warning signs are there; sometimes we learn the hard way and mark our own mental maps for the danger.

Our culture has some prevailing winds: rabid individualism, materialism, affluenza, addiction to addictions. It does not matter how big my spiritual engine is, or how strong my personal braking system is; if I am not grounded, the prevailing winds will push me out of my chosen path, and that oncoming Winnebago will show up, horn blaring.

Escape

I was looking for a way through.

I was riding down a major arterial in my neighborhood. It was a sunny, dry morning and traffic was light. Stopped at the next side street on my right was our local letter carrier. His name is Gerry. He is a friend of mine. I always smile when I see him in his postal truck. He is a good man and a good presence in our neighborhood. He knows me, and my bikes. As I came up on him, I smiled—I had my visor up. He was looking right at me.

I thought we made eye contact. I thought he smiled. I was wrong. Just as I approached the street, he pulled out—right in front of me—making a left turn onto the big street from the small street. I had one nanosecond to decide what to do before I hit the side of his truck.

When you are in motorcycle safety school (and no one should ride without this experience), they drum into your head that you must always be scanning the road ahead for potential dangers and potential solutions to those dangers.

The advantages of the bike over the cage are maneuverability and quicker acceleration/deceleration. We can go, stop and turn faster than you can. This is a simple fact of physics; much less mass, nearly equal power. This saves our lives—a lot.

One of our major disadvantages is visibility. We are smaller and your brain is accustomed to noticing cars and trucks, and often you just don't see us, even when you see us. This endangers our lives—a lot.

After alcohol and excess speed—both completely avoidable—the number one cause of motorcycle deaths is a car making a turn into your immediate path. This is unavoidable. It happens. But it is folly not to expect it. You make a mental discipline of presuming that you are either invisible, or that if you are visible, the vehicle ahead will intentionally attempt to kill you.

Making this presumption, you plan your way of escape. There is always a way of escape, usually more than one. You ride your bike in a manner that makes escape possible at any time. Then you get to live. Fail to plan your escape and you die.

On the day of my near-collision, I had four choices; none of them really good.

1. Swerve left—in front of his path. He might stop at the last second and I could scoot in front of him. I rejected this, as it is folly to bank on his seeing me, when he clearly had not seen me to this point.

2. Swerve right—and try and go behind him as he continued his left turn. This might work if he moved quickly enough, but it presumed that he would not see me at the last second and hit his brakes. In my experience, they often do see you at some point, and slamming on the brakes is always the natural response. I rejected this because it again, bet my safety on his response. I like to keep my safety in my own hands, whenever possible.

3. Try and make the right hand turn. Move onto the street that he was leaving. This could work if I did not have too much speed going into the turn. It would require lots of lean for my cruiser-style bike. If you fail, you go down into a slide, but that is preferable to hitting a large object directly. People survive slides. I was wearing good leathers.

4. Attempt the very fast emergency stop. If you are not going too fast, this often works. But if you lock up your brakes, you slide, often into or under the object you are trying to avoid. Going under a truck is not recommended.

There was not actually time to think through these options. These options had to be wired into my sinews and nerve endings.

I attempted a combo of three and four. He did see me at the last moment and he did slam on his brakes, coming to a stop, completely blocking the road in front of me. I turned to the right, leaned, and put the bike into a controlled sideways slide. I stood up, foot on my back brake and hand on the front brake. I was prepared to attempt to leave the bike if she went under the truck. I sacrificed a lot of good tire tread.

And I stopped, facing to the right, parallel to the truck, smack dab at Gerry's driver side window. I stood the bike upright. I had managed not to soil myself.

Gerry looked down at me and said "Expletive, Peg, expletive, I'm sorry. I did not expletive see you! Expletive!"

I looked up and said. "Expletive Gerry! Good thing I saw you! You almost expletive killed me! That would have sucked!"

Gerry: "No expletive!"

We were blocking traffic in two directions. He moved his truck across the street. I moved the bike to the side street. We both stayed put until we recovered. We did both recover.

This is yet another set of motorcycle truths that easily move into the spiritual realm. Don't travel so fast that you don't have time to deal with emergencies. Scan your horizon for trouble, but do it with a calm, relaxed, open attitude–fear and panic are not your friends. Always look for the way of escape–it is always there.

The Apostle Paul talks to the folks in Corinth about this. He says, "There is not a situation that will test you that is not natural and common. God is faithful and fair. You will not be tested above your skill level. With the test there always comes a way of escape." (1 Corinthians 10:13)

The word I have translated as test is often translated temptation, but test or trial is also a fair use of the Greek. So is assay, like checking the level of a precious metal. This passage is often preached narrowly as being about temptation to sin. And the take away is, you have no excuse for sin; there is always a way out.

This is a fair but limited exegesis. The implication is, if you sin, it is on you and you fail.

We do not learn without opportunities to test and use our skills. But we do not need to fear God as an assayer. God is not trying to catch us being bad; God is a fair educator who is on our side. Failure is a part of the learning curve and not to be feared. God gives us skills, the opportunities to use them, and a way to survive and thrive during the learning process. God made us, and knows that we have "the right stuff." God wants to use that stuff to whatever level we will take it.

With God, there is always a chance to retake the test.
With motorcycles, inattention can take away the re-test.

When the Bad Thing Happens

I have laid Rosie down at speed only once. It was up on the Puget Sound.

Maybe I should have worried when I went over the Tacoma Narrows Bridge–shaky territory. But when I realized I was on that fabled span, I rocked Rosie over and back and pretended the bridge was shaking. It was fun. I had a nice weekend at a picturesque retreat center with some Quakers. The bad thing happened when I turned around from the speck of a town called Seabeck and headed for home. It was a rainy day, and predicted to get worse. I had several hundred miles of interstate to ride home, so I lit out early on that Sunday morning.

I was barely on my way, riding in a slick and heavy mist on a narrow curvy road through a patch of Olympic rain forest. I was being cautious. I was maybe even going a bit slow, because I knew the curves would be treacherous with freshly lifted oil. The road was climbing as I approached a blind left-hand curve. I realized too late that it wasn't banked correctly. Then the tires went right out from under me. She laid down on her right side and slid. We were going fast enough that she slid up-hill and into the oncoming lane. I let go of her. It was that or my right leg was going under her. Somehow I managed to gain my feet and I ended up running a few steps uphill following her. Listening to metal and plastic scraping on pavement. She stopped just on the other side of the yellow line, and perpendicular to it. Her tires were higher than her seat or bars. I hit the kill switch and turned off her engine.

She weighs 500 lbs. On my best day, with a lot on adrenaline on board, I have a hard time picking her up (although I have done so.) But lifting her from a below-level position and up to vertical on a slick surface was just not going to happen and I knew it. As far as I know, angels don't schlepp.

I looked both ways for traffic. It had been very light. I could see back down the road behind me. No one coming. More concerning was the road ahead because I still couldn't see through the curve. All it was going to take was for a pick-up to come barreling through that curve and Rosie was going to be smithereens. Me too, considering where I was standing. And said truck wasn't going to be happy either. I should have gotten out of the road. Or more intelligently, I should have run ahead through the curve and tried to flag down anything that was coming. What I did was straddle my bike and put my arms out and waited for whatever was coming.

It didn't take long. I heard him before I saw him. The red Dodge truck came around that curve just like he was headed for home, which it turns out he was. He had a short moment to decide what to do. He missed us to the right by a couple of feet and sprayed gravel from the shoulder. I turned like a matador. He slid to a stop downhill and opened his door.

"My God, I almost killed you!"

"I live! And I need you to help me lift her before someone else comes around that bend!" I grabbed her bars and arranged her as he came running up behind me."

"You are an effin crazy woman!"

"It's been said."

The combined adrenaline was plenty. She was rolled to the downside shoulder in no time. She only left a few bits in the road. Truck dude and I talked a couple minutes as we both calmed down. A quick check and it seemed to me that my steed would run. Her brake levers were twisted but I could grab them. One of her turn signal casings was busted, but the light itself was working. I told my killer-turned-rescuer that I was going to ride into the next little town and do a better check. I thanked him sincerely. He shook his head at me and wished me luck.

When the bad thing happens you may have to let go, but if you find yourself standing, stand and trust.

Stopping

I was on the freeway, close enough to the speed limit. Sunny spring day. Singing a song with my angels in the fabulous acoustics of the full-face helmet. The wind was singing along too, because it was warm enough that I had the face screen cracked half an inch for temperature moderation. Then the universe required that I stop. Immediately.

The request came in the form of a bumblebee, which managed to defy the air stream flowing over my aerodynamic head and make a solid eye-level hit at 70 miles an hour and yet live. Groggy but not stunned, it crawled into the only opening available for safe haven, my slightly open face shield. I felt it on my lower lip. I swallowed a yell and willed my mouth shut. I gave a mighty snort to try and expel it. It buzzed angrily like a throttle twist on a Japanese speed bike. I pushed my visor full open—but the air coming in glued the bug to my face. I turned my head. It crawled up from my chin, over my lips and across my cheek, then up and over my ear and into my hair. There was more buzzing and thrashing up there as it unsuccessfully tried to escape.

At that point, I pried my attention away from the bee and onto the road. I was in the middle lane of three; I needed to make a lane change and a prompt stop. I scanned ahead, behind, and to the side. I had lots of room. I signaled. I slowed, moved over, and slowed some more. I signaled, slowed and moved onto the shoulder. My back end fishtailed a little bit when the bee made an especially angry protest and I reflexively stomped on my brakes, locking them for a second. I lightened up. I came to a swift but controlled stop on the gravel.

I used the kill switch on the engine and had the buckles off of my chinstrap in record time. Off with the helmet. Loose the long hair. Shake. The bee left. I had not been stung.

The bee lived by God's own miracle. I lived because of a cool head and good habits. I ride with the intent of always keeping a good stopping distance between me and whatever is in front, and if possible, a similar space off my stern.

A good stopping distance is that space which allows for a graceful, safe deceleration. Speed increases the need for space. Poking along—not much required. Cruising at what I call "God Speed," I like the length of two semi-trailers. For cagers—you people in cars—the "two-second rule" applies. Use any non-moving object as the mark and count two full seconds from the time the car in front of you passes it until you pass the mark.

I like to have more space than that, before and behind. Now, I know that those of you who drive in urban environments have a greater challenge with this. Other vehicles do not want you to have this space and will move into any space six inches larger than their cage. In California, they will connect these spaces across three or four lanes and 'surf.' This increases your challenge, but the challenge to maintain the best possible safety bubble is still important.

I want as much space as I can have. The spaces in your life are just as important as the objects, maybe more. Because life sometimes puts a bee in your bonnet.

One day, all of us are going to get that final red light, that "pavement ends ahead" sign. It may come on suddenly, or we may see it coming for miles, but it will come. The end is not up to us, but how we do it is. We can go screeching into that end with our brakes locked and screaming, or we can execute a nice controlled stop. The way you have lived your life is going to determine how you die. I want to be able to pull over and hand the keys over with some dignity and grace.

Might as well practice stopping now.

Righteous Revolution

A lot of people think that motorcycles are about rebellion. It ain't so. At least, I don't know anyone who rides primarily for that reason. Marlon Brando started that trope with one movie line, but he's dead and the movie is mostly forgotten.

Rebellion isn't what keeps us moving. A lot more people, and many bikers, say it's about freedom. That is closer. But often that still refers to the lesser sort of Freedom from, (demands, jobs, phones, expectations etc). Getting away is a piece of it, but not really the best reason to ride. When you are doing it right, riding is about intrinsic authority–knowing your own mind. It is more about Freedom for something. Yes, you have to escape the people who say–not safe–not comfortable–not feminine–not whatever... But a negative reason to do something is never a good enough reason. We ride because it is right for us. Because we know what we need. Because riding helps us feel awake and alive. Feeling alive is just another way of staying close to God. He said, "I am the Way the Truth and the Life." He could have said, I am the Road, the Reality, and the Revival. A good ride, even a harrowing ride, leaves me spiritually refreshed, even if I am physically whipped.

When I met Alivia Biko, she was not well. She was on chemotherapy for some auto-immune issues that were clearly tied to a life of abuse and self-abuse. She had all the "I hate me" diseases. She was also a dear friend of Jesus and was trying to live into His promise that she could revive. The church and the doctors were trying to help. Really, they were. Best of intentions. They did her many kindnesses. But the church asked her to try and be healed of being a lesbian, or at the very least, stay closeted and single. The doctors wanted her on disability, and on chemo for systemic lupus. Chemo and a closet just ain't much fun. No kinda life at all. It almost killed her.

I showed up one day with a church lady friend of Liv's. Liv was pukin' her way through the latest round. It was a beautiful spring day and I rode to Newberg. The friend said that we should go visit the sick before we went out to lunch. I walked in sporting the black leather. Alivia asked about my ride. She had to lift her head off the sofa to ask. I told her about Rocinante.

She said "I used to ride, but I probably won't ever again."

I said, "Says who?"

The church lady friend cut me a look.

"Could you hang on to the back of mine?"

"I might puke on you."

"I could deal."

Alivia decided to ignore the doctors and the concerned church ladies and do something that felt like life to her. If her own best voice had said rest—that would have been one thing. But some very important piece of her did not want to rest, it wanted to ride. She listened to that voice. We took that ride up the curvy road to Bald Peak. Something woke up in Alivia that day.

Quakerism is a listening spirituality. The core idea is that God is not done talking and that God will speak to you individually. We balance that with community and wise counsel. But the community gets timid, and stuck, and sometimes stupid. Sometimes doctors focus on fighting diseases more than waking up the healing functions.

Listening is a balance. But you have to listen to that voice inside you first. If you get into the habit of hearing that voice, you have to be willing to obey it, even when it means transgressing everyone else's rules and ideas of what is right. That holy obedient transgression is not rebellion. It is the precise opposite of rebellion. It is righteous revolution.

Reconciliation

In the spring of 1997, Scotts Mills Friends released me from pastoral ministry. I had stayed two years instead of six weeks. The purpose of my release was to be commissioned to a traveling ministry. They figured if a quadruple murder could happen in their family and church, it could happen anywhere, and they were right. They were also right in thinking that the important message about how to predict, prevent and respond to family violence was not getting to rural and conservative churches and communities. So they asked me to go tell them.

Job one was to figure out how to talk about it in a way that people could hear. This was a translation project. So I took all the materials I had—mostly made by liberal, feminist, urban women's shelter kind of people—and I sat down with an old retired fundamentalist minister and I tried out truth bits on him. If smoke came out his ears, I tried again. Then he started handing me useful Bible verses. Soon I was ready to go.

Rocinante and I spent the next two years intermittently out on the road in Oregon, Washington and Idaho. Going to churches, high schools, and Rotary clubs. Anyone who would listen. And they did listen. I think a few lives were saved. I think much badness was prevented. I saw it as rescue work. I didn't talk much about reconciliation.

But a funny thing started happening: reconciliation started to flow in the wake of what I thought of as calling out evil and calling people to walk away. Some people got out of bad situations, but some people stood their ground and demanded that bad get better.

I was not in charge of which choice they made for themselves. I just laid some truth on the table and they applied as needed.

The most powerful message that I regularly gave on that tour was a message about how God sees us. How valuable we are. How we are created for beauty and power. I received it whole from the Spirit. I preached it to build up victims and inoculate children. I was unprepared for its power to melt abusers. Because their souls know truth when it is spoken. They know that they were born for goodness, too.

I always made it back to Scotts Mills for Christmas Eve and Easter Weekend. Good Friday was tough for a couple of years. Truly, those folks didn't need to spend any extra time on death. But one Good Friday, I got to thinking about the sacrificial lamb. *Agnus Dei, Qui tollis peccata mundi*—the Lamb of God that takes away the sin of this world. This is what John the Baptist shouted at Jesus on the banks of the Jordan. (And you think you have weird cousins!)

As a child, I was taught that sin was ugly and had to be paid for—that Jesus paid our tab to a God so beautiful and rigid that He couldn't even look at ugly, even if that ugly was his child being murdered. Jewish families get to deal with their sins once a year at Yom Kippur. Catholics used to go once a week, except the grandmas, who went every morning. Now they go "as needed." Holiness children like me were just supposed to feel guilty most of the time.

But as I started to try and figure out this Lamb, something didn't fit. I went into the Hebrew Scriptures for a look at the animal sacrifice system and found that a lamb was what a middle class family brought to the temple for the Day of Atonement. If you were poor you could get away with a dove or two; the priests brought a bull. But on the Day of Atonement, the lamb is not punished, not banished, not ugly. It was a goat that was chosen by lottery and burdened with the sins of the people and pushed out into the wilderness to a presumably bad fate.

Margaret Magee looked at the full ugly of sin. She saw her daughter and granddaughters taken apart with a shotgun on her front doorstep. She was holding the hand of one of them at the time. As soon as she was able, she moved back into that house with the pellet marks in its siding. The husband/father/family annihilator was sent to prison and died there by his own hand—finishing his work of cowardice. This one tiny genocide was an unrepayable loss. How could anything repay the losses of a thousand genocides, a million murders, sins uncountable?

Scotts Mills did what it could. It invested out of proportion to its size in the health of the remaining community and surrounding world. Turns out they were being just like their God.

I realized that I had been taught a scapegoat theology of the cross, mislabeled as theology of the Lamb. John did not say "Behold! the Scapegoat of God who is gonna get good and punished for your wickedness!" He could have, it would have made sense, but it is not what he said. That would be a whole 'nother way of thinking, almost another religion. The lamb is good and is invested in the community. The priestly class literally lived off the excess sacrifice. The lamb was your best stuff, which built up and supported the community. The lamb restored.

What God did in Jesus was to invest deeply, completely in humanity. Including joining us in death. The power of that investment made it possible to restore and break death itself. It didn't un-do the suffering, but it made it possible to get beyond the suffering.

Then came the really interesting question. Whose lamb was it anyway? God's Lamb. Why does Yahweh, the clean and mighty, need a lamb? The lamb is brought by the sinner, the one who wants to say sorry, and do better, and is willing to stop sinning and invest in that choice. Some would say because humanity didn't have a lamb good enough to satisfy. That we are ugly and Yahweh can't look at or accept ugly. This answer no longer satisfies me. Those babies in Scotts Mills were pure, whole, complete, lovely. I do not believe that we come into this world messed up. I believe we get messed up by living in it. In a world we did not make.

I think that the idea of God's Lamb is much more powerful than that. God knew that God needed to take the first step. Far from being angry with us, forgiveness actually precedes repentance. God has been moving towards us as a group and as individuals since the beginning. God is not put off by our sins, even the worst of them. God says, "Here, let me give you a hand out of that." Sin is what happens when we try and deal with stuff on our own. And maybe God takes some of the responsibility for this pickle we are in. Because we may be a mess, but we are God's mess, and God not only knows that, but acknowledges it. Because reconciliation is never one-way. And often the less culpable party has to take the first step.

"Forgive them, they don't know what they are doing!" Forgive whom? The Romans, the Sanhedran, the crowds, the not-so-impressed thief, the dude with the hammer in his hand. Did Jesus insist that they repent before he forgave them? He did not.

Scotts Mills pulled themselves up out of their grief and sacrificed to invest in the world. And they were healed. Bearing scars, for sure, but able to celebrate Easter again, and Christmas, to trust again in the predominant goodness of the world. And they, the victims, had to take the first steps, because the abusers sure weren't going to be the ones to start it. I was amazed out on the road, how many times the abusers responded to those strong, truthful, but infinitely gracious first steps. The exception, certainly, not the rule, but real each time.

This was all working through me, but it worked above a great, unsettled quagmire. I was once again about to get caught up in my own preaching. A test of good preaching is that the preacher has as much to learn from it as anyone else. If they have something all figured out, then the words are from them, human. Maybe good teaching, but just that. If it is a message from You Know Who, it will knock the excuses right out from under the preacher, just like anyone else.

I went to the summer gathering of Friends the third summer after the murders. They had me talk to the whole group. I had been once again carefully avoiding the pastors, a couple, from the church who had beat me bloody and sent me running—the one before Scotts Mills. I figured it was kindness to just not see those people. I think they were also doing a good job of avoiding me. But it wasn't that big a gathering, and the inevitable happened one evening. My former co-worker and I ended up at the sinks in the ladies room. We both stopped and stared in the mirror. I saw the woman who had betrayed me and passed on slander. She saw the woman who had threatened to sue her.

I said, "We should talk—we really should talk—I'm willing to talk."

She said, "OK, when?"

"How about tomorrow, then your husband can join us."

And we agreed on a time and a place.

I stayed up all night praying. I really did not want to forgive these people. I really did not want to hear a bunch of rationalizations for what they did. And I REALLY did not want to take any responsibility for my reasonable and assertive actions that probably scared them silly.

Sometime deep in the night, still on my knees, I slipped into a dream or a vision. I was in a very futuristic train station. A guide was at my right shoulder. I told the guide that I wanted this over, and that I didn't really want to do it, but that I believed that I should. I thought it was going to be ugly and not likely to get to the desired result.

The guide said. "It is not a required trip, but if you want to get to there, it is easier to do the last station first."

"What, forgive them first and see if they repent?"

"Yes, but repentance is over-rated."

"Ok, how do we do that?"

"We should see the clerk of the station first."

And we went over to an elevator, and went down to about the 42nd sub-basement, and stepped into an office, with a book on a desk.

"What did they do to you?" said the guide. And I named how I had been hurt.

And the book fluttered its pages, and then stopped.

"There it is." said the guide. "Do you want it to be erased?"

And I found that I did.

And the page was empty.

"That's it?"

"Yes, it's easy when you are ready, just paperwork. I think we had better get going, I hear your train coming." We took the elevator back up and in pulled a shiny silver bullet train and I got on." And I was back in my room. I wanted coffee.

I met with that woman (her husband chose not to come.) It wasn't comfortable, but it wasn't hard. I started, and described what I thought those bad days must have been like for her. This is important. I didn't ask her to listen to my pain, I didn't need her to ratify my reality. I tried to climb into hers. She did the same for me. Neither of us got it quite right, but we tried. I didn't need anything from her. I gave her a gift of empathy. She gave in kind, rather than requiring anything of me. Then I told her that I forgave her and I asked her to forgive me, and it didn't hurt at all. Because the Lamb we both claimed to serve had already laid all the groundwork for this. I haven't actually seen her since that day, but I could. I bear her no ill will. She didn't make the mess she was in. Neither did I. If I ever meet the young fellow whose choices made life so difficult for me that year, I could forgive him too. I bet he didn't make his mess either. I feel pretty sure that God is sorry that we all had to go through it. So God did something about that.

Part 3:
Deep in the Heart of Texas

The cross-country motorcycle saga is an American archetypal story. Almost every biker gets around to having their own there-and-back-again quest, and the American West, in particular offers enormous spaces that are relatively safe to travel. The journey usually involves fully testing your limits, facing adversity, chance meetings and help from unexpected quarters. It always changes the rider. If you are a narrative theologian who happens to ride, the Odyssean nature of the thing gets overlaid with Biblical import. My chance came when Rosie and I had been together for about five years.

The Annunciation

A scant thirty second gap separated my initial reaction from the thought that followed–and that gap was the only chance uncertainty ever had. As soon as the next thought appeared in that thirty-first second, the whole thing was a done deal.

My initial reaction was in response to the invitation I opened that day in November 1996. I was being asked to speak at the National Wesleyan/Holiness Women's Clergy Conference in San Antonio, Texas in the spring of 1998. My exact reaction was, "Me and 600 Holiness Women? Not Likely... not in this lifetime!" Thirty seconds later, the next thought arrived; "San Antonio, Texas... in April. Oh dear, Jesus Christ has just given me a 5,000 mile, tax deductible, motorcycle ride!!!" After that, everything else was follow-through.

The thought of this trip pleased me a great deal. I did season the idea a bit, quietly grinning at odd moments. But when my family had just about decided that I had gone daffy, I set about the task of gathering what I needed for the journey.

The first two requirements were the blessings of those closest to me, and the curses of a few not-so-close ones. In my world, in order to accomplish something really difficult, I like to have at least three people tell me that I cannot do it. I am almost mature enough these days that if someone knowledgeable tells me that a thing can't be done, I slow down and listen. But if someone says, "It can be done, but YOU can't do it," I head straight into the Eat My Dust Zone. It seemed to me that this project was going to require that sort of motivation.

Obtaining the blessings of my husband, and my father, who lived with us, was not too hard. At first, I think they didn't believe me. "Texas? Well, be careful and have fun" was pretty much the reaction I received. My nearest and dearest learned long ago never to say "can't" to me. But, as we all know, a blessing is a blessing, even if given without much thought; just ask Esau. (The Old Book–Genesis 27)

Gathering the necessary cant's turned out to be a little harder. When in the spring of '97, I started saying publicly that I would be riding to Texas in a year, I mostly garnered stunned silences. Sometimes these silences were followed by the short question, "Alone?" and then another stunned silence. Fortunately, about that time, my older brother, (a historically steady source of "cant's" in my life), came through with the first one, and that got things rolling. The next two came in quick succession from a church lady, who shall remain nameless, and my insurance agent. I was all motivated up.

Prepare Ye the Way

The following months were filled with lots of map studying, route planning, and weather research. Late April is dicey in the mountain ranges and high plains that I would have to cross before I would get to the southlands and warm weather. Once in Texas, I would run smack dab into the beginning of tornado season. In any direction, I would have at least three mountain ranges to cross.

Getting out of the state of Oregon, from my Willamette Valley home in Salem, means getting over the Cascades to the east, or over the Siskiyous to the south. The Cascades are higher and more persistently snowy, even into May and sometimes June. Interstate 5, which runs the length of the west coast, passes over the Siskiyou Mountains, and is more passable year round, with only a few months of mandatory chains and occasional brief closures. But if I went south, my next chance to turn east would be over the Sierra Nevada Range, and the phrase "Donner Party" kept springing to mind.

The only truly weather-safe route would be 1,000 miles straight south to Los Angeles on I-5, then 1,500 miles due east on I-10 to Texas. This route would add many miles to my ride and it would be ugly, tedious, and not necessarily safer. Personally, I think that I would rather face a mishap on Donner Pass than on the Santa Monica Freeway. If I took a more northerly route, over the Cascades, then the Rockies awaited me; not exactly mountain range sissies. Any way I went from Salem, snow looked possible, and wind and cold rain were pretty much a certainty.

I eventually settled on three possible routes. If God was very weather-gracious to me and all was clear, I would cross the mountains to the east, go down the back side of the Cascades into northern Nevada, over to Salt Lake, across the canyon lands to cut off the corner of Colorado and the Rockies, down into New Mexico and then diagonally across the state of Texas to San Antonio. If things were a little colder, I would leave Oregon by the south gate and then try and zip around the south side of Mt. Shasta into Nevada, diagonally cross that state to Hoover Dam and into Arizona, then cut across that state and pick up I-10 where New Mexico meets Old Mexico. If things were really bad, well, to paraphrase an old Irish blessing, "May you get out of L.A. thirty minutes before the Devil finds out you have arrived."

I had determined a start date of Friday April 17, 1998, with a one-day window of flexibility on either side, so I could leave when the weather was best. I was expecting to need to time my departure between spring storms. I was planning to make it in five days' riding time with a planned spare sixth day for mechanical trouble, needed rest, injury, weather delays or unforeseen circumstances. If things went well, I was hoping to take a little side trip to the Grand Canyon.

This time line had me arriving in San Antonio late on Wednesday the 22nd. The conference was to start on the 23rd, and I wasn't scheduled to speak until Saturday morning the 25th. So even figuring in disaster, I might be late for the start, but wouldn't miss my talk. After four days of Holiness, I would turn for home and arrive back in Salem on or about Friday May 1st. I was hoping that in those two weeks, the weather would continue to warm and I could take a northern route home. I had scheduled several days of nothing at the beginning of May, to either come home slowly if need be, or to recuperate when I arrived.

Horse and Rider

In the spring of 1998, even though Rocinante was in nearly mint condition, I took her to the motorcycle doctor for a thorough check-up. New tires were bought; oil, battery, all that. There had been one balky moment the previous winter when she stalled at speed on I-5, but it never repeated and I chalked it up to winter funkiness. My mechanic, Bill, stated that she was "good to go" for 5,000 miles. Her only handicap is a 3.2 gallon gas tank. This is about 130 miles at full throttle, or what I like to call "Godspeed." It is a real risk to go beyond where the reserve kicks in at about 120 miles, and both my first and second route choices had several 150-mile stretches without gas. Then there is always the chance that they will have closed the only gas station in Podunk, Utah when you get there.

I started to think about ways to carry a bit of gas externally on the bike. I may have harbored secret doubts about my own ability to pull this off; but my machine I never doubted.

I arranged for a Road Service called Mow Tow that would come get you anywhere in the U.S. I got a cell phone.

In January, I started to prepare my body. At the time of this ride, I was a 41 year-old mother of two. For the first time in my life, I headed for a gym. My trip plan required me to be able to ride five consecutive 500-mile days. Previously, the longest one-day ride I had ever taken was a little over 600 miles, and I spent the next day in bed. The most consecutive days I had ridden was three, and my best combination was 1400 miles in five days (San Francisco and back). A 500 mile day takes at least seven hours; ten with breaks.

In late April, I would have at maximum twelve and a half hours of daylight. Horsing around the 500 pound bike for ten hours a day requires strength and stamina. I started to lift weights.

It's not Heavy, It's My Luggage

Anyone who has ever traveled with me or ever carried my luggage on a weekend trip (you know who you are, God bless you) knows that the first and perhaps the greatest miracle of this trip was solving the obvious luggage problem. Rosie has two semi-permanent saddlebags that hold about one cubic foot total. To this I added the largest commercially made, strap-on bike bag I could find. This bag is essentially a backpack for the motorcycle that sits on the passenger seat behind the rider and makes a nice backrest. It holds about two cubic feet of stuff and comes with an optional top-roll that adds another foot. So I had available to me four cubic feet of space to carry everything that Rosie and I would need for the journey. The problem was that motorcycling in hot and cold weather requires completely different wardrobes, and attending a Holiness conference obviously would require yet another. There would be no time for doing laundry on the road, and Rocinante would have some very serious requirements of her own. I can pack four cubic feet for an afternoon picnic.

I thought, rethought, collected opinions both mechanical and fashion, and started to collect the needed gear. I worried a bit when the collection started to fill a spare room in my house. I practiced packing and re-packing the bags. I made adjustments. I prayed. And at last, on me, or on Rosie, were the following items.

- 6" St. Michael the Archangel statue
- compass and dash clock
- epoxy glue kit
- 2 qt. spare gas can
- metric socket set
- needlenose pliers
- vise grips
- 4 screwdrivers (phillips & straight)
- Leatherman's tool
- tire repair kit w/ CO_2 cartridges
- duct tape/ electrician's tape
- chain & cable & locks
- 1 qt. synthetic oil
- 4 in 1 oil
- rags
- octane booster
- siphon hose
- fuses & spare light bulbs
- flashlight
- can of lemon Pledge
- owner's manual
- laminated maps
- extensive first aid kit
- spare face shield
- cell phone
- pocket knife
- assorted bungee cords
- cowboy boots
- 2 pairs jeans: blue/black
- 7 turtlenecks
- 2 T-shirts
- 1 fuzzy sweater
- 10 pairs socks
- various foundational garments
- thermals
- sweatpants
- silk pajamas
- tank top
- swimming suit
- silk jacquard dress
- 3 skirts
- red linen blazer
- raw silk natural blazer
- 3 dress sweaters
- red pumps/black pumps
- pantyhose & spare
- large make-up bag
- blow dryer
- curling iron
- bag of lotions & potions
- small towel
- journal
- Day Timer
- Gore-Tex 2-pc rain suit
- light riding gloves
- winter gloves
- electrically heated gloves
- a traveling minute

Anticipation

By April of '98, I was pretty much ready, planned, packed and prepared. Rosie was champing at the bit. I would walk through the garage most days and pat her on the saddle, whispering, "Soon, soon." By this point, everyone believed that I was really going. Father and husband had done a little bit of panicking. Father offered to buy me plane tickets, thinking that I was driving to save money. I'm not sure he knew I was planning on spending three grand on a three C-note gig. They recovered, and resigned themselves to the inevitable.

Then came the last bit of serendipitous, psychological encouragement. Dick Sartwell, pastor of Newberg Friends Church called and, not knowing about my trip, invited me to preach all three services at the Newberg, Oregon church on Sunday, May 3.

Now, you have to understand: this is the Mother Church, the genesis spot of Northwest Yearly Meeting of Friends. Being asked to preach there is like getting the call to the Majors. It's like being offered the big room at Caesar's Palace. Dick wanted me to preach a middle sermon in his series on the Apocalypse of John. Cool stuff. And I had never, ever, turned down a chance to preach the Gospel, except for a previously scheduled preaching gig.

I explained my travel plans to Pastor Sartwell–told him that I was due back in the state less than 36 hours before he needed me, and that was if all went well. I pointed out that a problem as small as a flat tire could cause me to miss the morning, and perhaps without much notice. I let him choose. Being the great gambler that he is, he took the odds, and bet on me and my horse. What a guy!

I took this as a Divine omen that I was going to live through this thing. I now had the final missing piece to my personal success formula—time pressure—a pot of gold at the end of the rainbow—a deadline. I have always done my best work under deadline.

A Blessing

All was ready the second week of April, except the weather. Spring was coming late. It was snowing in the Cascades. It was snowing in the Siskiyous. It was snowing in the Sierra Nevadas. It was snowing in Salt Lake, Colorado and New Mexico. I was on the phone and the internet; watching reports, looking at satellite photos. Everything to the east was bad. The weekend before I was to leave, an acquaintance drove up from California and was stopped at Siskiyou summit on the Oregon-California border for six hours waiting for the snow plows to clear the Pass. The Wednesday before "Big Friday", things were improving to the south, but ice was still being reported on I-5.

Thursday broke sunny and beautiful; the weather reports were still advising chains, but the daytime temps were encouraging. I called the Super-8 Motel in Susanville, California–my hoped-for first night stop on route B and talked to my first angel, a kind soul named Eris. I explained to her what I was up to and asked her about the road around Mt. Shasta. She said "Honey, there's lots of snow on the sides of the road, but you'll get through. You come on down, you're gonna be just fine." I chose to believe her.

Thursday afternoon, I packed Rocinante and we went over to see my Spiritual Director, Marcile Crandall. Out on the pavement in front of her house, I knelt with my helmet under my arm, she put one hand on my head and one on Rosie, and she gave us this ancient Irish blessing:

May the Cross of the Son of God who is mightier than all
the hosts of Satan, and more glorious than all the angels of
Heaven, abide with you in your going out and your coming in!

By day and by night, at morning and at evening, at all times and in all places, may it protect and defend you! From the wrath of evil men, from the assaults of evil spirits, from foes invisible, from the snares of the devil, from all low passions that beguile the soul and body, may it guard, protect and deliver you. In the name of the Father, and the Son, and the Holy Spirit. Amen!

Well, if that didn't cover it all, I don't know what would. We were ready. I ate a good meal with my family, went to bed early, and slept well. Ready.

On the First Day

I said good-bye to my husband at first light. Dad walked me out to the driveway when I was ready. A woman walked by and said, "Looks like you're going on a long ride."

"Texas," I replied. "Well! Ride safe!" she said, starting an unbroken chain of stranger-blessings. Not once, in the next fourteen days, did anyone on the road, ever, say anything negative to me about the ride. Which is unusual, as people often seem to feel perfectly comfortable telling me that I am crazy and that I should go home. For the duration, gas station attendants clapped me on the back and said, "You go get 'em," waitresses brought me free dessert and said, "Don't you worry 'bout a thing sweetie–you're bein' taken care of," and truck drivers said, "The road's gonna' be very good to you, keep goin'." I was blessed, mile by mile.

The day warmed up and I flew along the southbound road. My mood was high and all things seemed possible. I made Grants Pass by noon and stopped for lunch with a friend. It felt safe and fun and hardly like an adventure at all.

After lunch, Rosie was just humming, so to keep her company, I sang. I started warming up for Texas with all my favorites by Willie Nelson and Lyle Lovett. A bit of Lyle's lyrics kept coming to me: "My Angel in distress, you look OK to me, I'll send you my address, when I know what it will be...." Distress seemed far away.

I made the California border by 2 pm. There was snow on the hills to either side of me, but the sun was shining and the temperature was in the mid-50s and the road was dry. At 3 pm, I left I-5, turned east, and headed up, to go around Mt. Shasta.

The air got crisp. I stopped and added a sweater and my electrically heated gloves (a wonderful invention— like toasters on your hands). The mountain was spectacular, doing a moving-mountain dance in and out of a haze. I saw my first eagle. There was lots of snow, often 8-10 foot drifts at the side of the road. For one stretch of a mile or so, I ran through what felt like a tunnel of snow—15-20 feet on each flank—ponderosa pines buried to half their height. But like Moses through a frozen white sea, I passed through on a small path of pavement that was always at least a plow's width, wet but clear. I passed frozen meadows and lakes and then started coming down the other side.

Once on the downward side, I asked a woman in a rest stop ladies room if she'd take a photo of me with the bike and snow. When she walked away with me across the parking lot, her concerned husband popped out of their car and came running after us. "It's OK honey," she called, "I just need to help this lady motorcycle preacher—Nobody in Texas is going to believe that she rode through snow to get to them."

The sun fell behind the mountains as I rode into Susanville. Eris came out of the Super-8 to meet me. "Bout time you got here!—Got your bed ready, honey—The special tonight at the cafe is real good—Look at you!—all covered with mud—I'll get some rags—can't have you using my good towels to clean your gear."

Four hundred eighty-six miles, two mountain ranges, one day. I was tired and hungry; but happy, proud of myself, and full of confidence.

Dancing With the Angels, While the Lions Roar

I awoke on Day Two feeling good. But it was 34 degrees outside at eight am, so I delayed my departure for an hour and had coffee and doughnuts with Eris while the sun warmed things up a bit. I got out of Susanville at about nine.

The ride that morning was glorious; wide-open rangeland dotted with ponderosa pines, horizons galore. I started what became an every morning practice on the ride–worship sharing with my angels.

I have become increasingly aware of the spiritual comrades who ride with me–a small cohort who watch, witness, encourage, guide and protect. They do not replace that inner voice that I know belongs to my Shepherd. They are clearly external, but present to me. I occasionally feel their tug of guidance, their buffer zone of protection, their muffled joy, their keen awareness of danger. They enrich and amplify my awareness of Christ.

Often on the road, I would be asked if I was traveling alone. At first, it was my custom to reply, "No, I'm riding with angels." But soon I discovered that this caused people to look nervously around for a gang of Hells Angels. "No, no" I would say, "Not those angels–the other ones–the good guys." But I ended up shelving the whole response.

Worship sharing is a Quaker way of experiencing God with others. A group sits together in silence, and then at the prompting of the Spirit, each one shares out of the silence, a word, or thought, or prayer. That morning we weren't sitting still, we were flying along towards the Nevada border, but we had a blessed time anyway. We started things out by singing, "Holy, Holy, Holy" (a biggie on the angel hit-parade) in four part harmony. Then we enjoyed some wind-whipped silence, and then my comrades shared with me. They showed me a freight train in the distance. I guessed it to be about fifty cars long, but because the panorama was so huge, this entire, massive, train took up only a couple inches of the horizon. They whispered to me, "We see your life like that—an unbroken whole. You are lovely and complete." My question about whether I was near the engine or the caboose of my life went unanswered. I had nothing to show them except the contents of my heart, full of joy and gratitude.

I have a six-inch plastic St. Michael, wings unfurled and sword held overhead glued to Rosie's tiny dashboard. I keep him there to remind me that I should never ride faster than my angels can fly. I guess I should have worried when St. Michael unglued himself and tried to crawl off the bike, precisely at the Nevada state line. I stopped, got out my 5-minute epoxy, and glued him back on.

Then, two miles inside the state, Rosie sputtered, choked and died at speed. I pulled over; she restarted immediately, and seemed fine. I proceeded and had no trouble through Reno. I stopped in Sparks, Nevada, for a big brunch. They actually have a huge sign out there that says, "Reno—so close to Hell you can see Sparks."

Nevada is a weird place; "Addictions-R-Us" seems to be the state motto. Every little gas station is wall-to-wall hard liquor; they might have one Coke and a musty old bag of chips for sale, but every other square inch of floor space is booze. Bathrooms have slot machines. What is written on the stalls, even in the ladies' rooms, is amazing. Frankly, I don't like the whole scene.

My plan called for me to go east of Reno and then catch a back road that went due south through the desert to Las Vegas. I figured that without trouble, I had just enough time to make Las Vegas by dark. I had reservations waiting for me. This route took me through a little town called Fallon. Fallon sits at the end of one long straight stretch, and just before another. It is one of those towns you can see coming.

I saw it, and I started to slow from the legal 75 mph limit—then I saw the sign posting a sudden 25—then I saw Brother Law Enforcement Officer sitting right behind the sign. He also saw me. I had just enough time to get her down to 38 when he pulled out and pulled me over.

Unbeknownst to me, there was a large contingent of bikers from San Francisco reported to be heading through this part of Nevada for a desert rendezvous. Apparently, Brother Officer had been waiting all day for them. He was frustrated. I was going to have to do. He was a little surprised when the helmet came off and his lone renegade turned out to be a lady.

"You headin' out to meet those boys over in Laughlin?"

"No sir, I'm going south; due to stop in Las Vegas tonight on my way to Texas."

"You're goin' to Texas all by yourself?"

(I wisely refrained from the angel remark.)

"Yessir."

"And just why would you be goin' to Texas?"

"Well, sir, I'm going to San Antonio to preach the Gospel."

"Uh-huh." (At this point he ran my license, and came back disappointed that I was not a felon in Fallon.)

"Exactly what are you doing again, Missy?"

At this point, I asked and received permission to get into my bag, and I retrieved my traveling minute—a sort of Quaker ID—an explanation of a ministry that my home meeting addressed to any meeting or individual that I might encounter.

"This, sir, is my letter of introduction; I am a traveling Quaker minister, on a mission."

SCOTTS MILLS FRIENDS CHURCH
Post Office Box 56
520 Grandview Avenue
Scotts Mills, Oregon 97375
(503) 873-5526

April 3, 1998

Dear Friends,

We commend Peggy Parsons to your fellowship and care. She is a traveling evangelist and minister of the Lord, active in preaching and spiritual direction in her vocation, our meeting, and Northwest Yearly Meeting. She is traveling via motorcycle from April 17th to May 3rd. In San Antonio, Texas, April 23rd-26th, she will be speaking at the Wesleyan/Holiness Women Clergy Conference, carrying our concern for the church to actively address the problem of family violence. Peggy has been the Lord's special gift to us, and we invite you to know her as well.

Sincerely,

Jeanne Hazel
Presiding Clerk
Scotts Mills Friends Church

He scratched his head, read my minute, scratched his head again and looked at me over the top of his mirrored sunglasses.

"Well, this is the Gol-darndest thing I ever did see, but I got a feeling I had better not give you a ticket today."

He then warned me about the bikers, and carefully explained to me the concept of a speed trap.

"See Missy, you gotta slow down at the first sight of a town, we-all are out here waitin' for the likes of you, an' you're gonna get stopped in every town from here to Texas if you don't slow down."

He told me where to get good gas on my route that day and rode me sedately out of town. As I headed out into the desert, it was two in the afternoon and I had three hundred miles to cross before bed. I thought my luck was improving.

Providence, Nevada

There is a whole lot of nothing out on Route 95. It runs between several Air Force testing grounds and the California border, with Death Valley just on the other side. The scenery is remarkable, if you like stark and barren. There are about three towns out there, two just big enough to have a gas station. At one station I actually had to crank the pump manually.

In the largest of the towns, there is a place called the Mozart Piano Bar. On the side of the building is a painting of a skeleton, and a caption reads, "This guy drank water." The notion of Wolfgang Amadeus Mozart reincarnated in a honky-tonk in Nowhere, Nevada, tickled my funny bone. In the smaller town, there is a man who has a yard collection of dragsters, VW Bugs, an airplane and a sign that declares "Nothing for sale." Nevadans seem big on pithy signs.

The longest stretch of road was about 150 miles of serious nothing. At four p.m. I was about halfway across this stretch when Rosie choked again. Full throttle, then just a hint of warning in the form of an acceleration loss, then dead nothing. I coasted to a stop, and she started, but choked again. I got out my cell phone to test my emergency system. I wasn't ready to call Mow Tow for a ride yet, but I wanted to know that they were there.

This is when I learned a fundamental lesson about cell phones. They don't work without a cell tower. I was deep in the middle of No Service Land. If the Air Force was out there listening in Area 51, they weren't answering. Rats.

I took out my spare two quarts of gas and filled the tank—pure superstition, as she had half a tank in her, but it seemed to cheer her up a bit. She started and stayed started. We took off, but at full open throttle the best she could give me was 25 mph. I started up a long hill, just waiting for her to stop again.

I was contemplating what I was going to do if she stopped for good. It was too far to walk. I could not imagine abandoning my bike and gear and hitching a ride into Vegas, but waiting all night in the desert cold for a state trooper, who probably wouldn't come, didn't seem like a good idea either. There were no ranches out there, and I hadn't seen another vehicle ahead or behind me for at least 30 miles. I started to pray, and I prayed hard.

Then we topped the ridge and I was looking out over a huge caldera valley. And lo and behold, as they say, there out in the middle of the valley were a whole bunch of people and cars. As I got closer I saw that there were motorcycles! Dirt bikes out in the middle of the desert, racing in circles.

As I came down the hill, I could see the nearest group. Sitting there by the side of the road, like a mirage, was a semi-trailer that read "Team Kawasaki–Race Team 1." I was dumbstruck, but I swear I heard the angels laughing. It started to sink in that there in the middle of the stinking desert, within one mile of where my Kawasaki had trouble, were the best Kawasaki mechanics on the planet.

Right about then, she died again. I put her in neutral and aimed myself at the mechanics. It was a long coast down the hill. I rolled on in like a pit stop at Indy, only silent as a ghost. Now, if I was surprised to see these guys, then I have to say that they were at least as surprised to see me, especially coming in at full speed without engine noise.

Turned out they were testing new bikes against Team Honda and some others. They had finished for the day, and they had won. They were celebrating, with enthusiasm. A dozen guys, most in their early twenties, gathered around me. Now, motorcycle mechanics run the same gamut of humanity as everyone else, some are bad characters and some are genuinely nice folks, but as a lot, they are not particularly known for their couth or communication skills.

I stopped Rosie in the dust and whipped off the helmet. I was grinning like an idiot at my good fortune, and they were grinning like idiots at the sight of me. Their first attempt at communication was to offer me the Jim Beam. I thanked them and declined. I started to try and get across my predicament.

After a little good-natured jesting they tried to listen to my description of the mechanical trouble. Then, just as I got to the part about the acceleration loss, they all, to a man, fell over laughing. I mean hysterics. I had absolutely no idea what I had said that was so funny. So I waited, and the most mature of the lot finally pulled himself together and said this:

"We know what's wrong with your bike."

"Great," I said. "Is it fixable?"

"Oh yeah, no problem."

" What's wrong?"

"Well, Lady, (laughter) you got problems with your petcock."

(More riotous laughter all around.)

"I didn't actually know I had a pet cock," said I.

(Now they are on the ground again.)

You may not think this is all that hilarious, but then, dear reader, you are not, thank Goodness, a drunken motorcycle mechanic. Eventually, I found out that there is a spring-loaded vacuum valve between the gas tank and the carburetors, called the petcock, which stops or starts the flow of gas. If this valve becomes jammed for any reason, gummed up or vapor locked, no gas flows and you stop. The cure, oddly enough, was to open the gas tank and depressurize the tank. If this failed, you got off the bike, knelt by the side of the engine, unhooked a vacuum hose and sucked and blew the line clean.

The Kawasaki boys made sure that they instructed me in this practice and seemed to enjoy the spectacle. They checked out the rest of the bike, found me a plain old Coke somewhere, topped off

Rosie's gas tank again and assured me that I would get to Vegas. They sent me off with a big cheer. All in all, they were nice fellows, if a bit crude. Never say that our God does not have a sense of humor, or cannot use whomever He chooses.

As I topped the next rise, I had the distinct feeling that if I turned around, that the desert would be empty. If I had seen Rod Serling in a Twilight Zone pose by the side of the road, I would not have been surprised. But then I bet those poor guys woke up the next morning with headaches and not sure if that woman on the silent Vulcan had really ridden in to camp yesterday afternoon.

Rosie seemed fine for the next fifty miles. It was a good thing that they had topped off my tank because I rode into civilization on fumes. The first chance for gas was, no kidding, a combination gas station/bordello. I was ready to get out of Nevada.

It was dark and cold before I made Las Vegas. My hotel was down on the Strip and I was not in the mood. Nothing drains a body like fear. Traffic was deadly, five lanes each way and Saturday night crazy. I was exhausted, mentally and physically. I got lost, and then found my way. My hotel was huge and it was clear that I was going to have to leave Rosie in a casino parking lot, which meant I would have to strip her of all her gear to keep it from being stolen. To top it all off, the parking lot was full of drunken Air Force cadets, and I was really not in the mood to deal with them. I was not even feeling good about leaving the bike. But I had nowhere else to go.

Just then, the only sober man in Nevada showed up. He looked like Mr. T—huge, black, bald, muscled, bejeweled, and thank God, the hotel security man. When I told him I was a guest, he showed me a better parking spot where there was a post to which I could chain the bike's front and rear tires. He told me to leave the saddlebags full of tools, and that he would watch her for me. He radioed in to the desk clerk and asked her to give me a room overlooking that part of the lot. Then he said, "Don't worry, you're right where you're supposed to be—get some sleep. Things will look better in the morning."

I hadn't told him a thing about my day. I was totally spooked by this point. But I shouldered my load and got my room. I looked out the window and there he was, like Mr. Clean, standing by my bike. He grinned and waved to me. I smiled weakly and waved back.

I fell into bed. Too tired to eat, too tired to shower. I got up twice in the night, disoriented and anxious, and both times when I looked out the window, there he was, within sight; both times, he looked up and smiled.

Sabbath

Sunday morning, I woke out of disorganized dreams into disorientation. When I remembered where I was, I looked outside; Rosie seemed fine, but my guard was gone. I said a Sabbath prayer and asked for guidance. The Kawasaki boys out in the desert had suggested that perhaps I had gotten something in my gas to clog the petcock valve or the gas tank screen. They thought I should have the tank taken off and cleaned in Las Vegas, but they weren't thinking about being in Las Vegas on a Sunday morning. Nothing is open except the perpetual casinos. (Oddly enough, the wedding chapels close on Sunday mornings.)

I went through an extensive Yellow Pages listing and found not one motorcycle repair shop that would be open that day. I was loath to start across Arizona without a little more confidence, but I finally decided that if I could find a five-gallon gas can, I could drain the tank myself and lift the tank enough to check the screen.

I found a parts store that would be open at ten. I loaded the bike, and had a big, cheap, smoky breakfast off the lobby casino. About 9:30 in the morning, I headed out to find the parts shop and waited for them to open.

A guy named Dave showed up. I tried to buy a gas can (I had my own siphon), and asked him if he would mind me working on my bike in his parking lot. He asked me what I was up to, and I gave him the whole story. I found out that he was the owner of the shop and that he had grown up in his father's Kawasaki dealership. Even though his store had no service bays, he rolled my bike into the back of his store. He had tire-changing equipment there, and in between customers he drained my tank, cleaned the petcock and screen, and blew the whole system clean with compressed air. We discovered that the cap on my little spare gas can was degrading and sending flecks of plastic into the system. The can went in the trash, and Rosie got fresh gas.

I have to tell you that it was pretty scary to see my steed taken apart by someone I didn't know, a thousand miles from home and fifteen hundred miles from my destination. But sometimes the middle of a miracle can seem pretty dark—just ask Jonah.

At 2 p.m., Dave sent me on my way. He refused to write up the job or accept money for the three hours of motorcycle maintenance. He told me that he had two little boys at home and asked me to pray for them. I put a real good blessing on them and their daddy.

I headed out of Las Vegas to the southeast and went over the Hoover Dam. I hadn't thought about the Sunday afternoon tourists, so actually, we crawled over the Dam. I could have walked faster, but it gave me a good look. Hoover Dam impressed me as an amazing insertion of human works into God's work. Enormous, but oddly precarious, looking as if at any time Nature might take back her own. As I rode over into the state of Arizona, I was grateful that God is skilled at joining us in our work, even if we don't return the favor.

I had a nice hundred-mile stretch of desert to let Rosie loose on, and she seemed very happy. She got 47 miles to the gallon riding into Kingman. We were all glad to be safely out of Nevada.

Samurai Road Warriors

On the morning of day four, the idea of adventure was wearing a bit thin. I had used up my spare day. A Grand Canyon excursion was out. Half of my allotted time was gone, and I would not reach the halfway mileage point for several hundred miles. But the sun was shining and the weather was warming –50 degrees at start time. So determination took over where adventure-seeking ended.

I treated myself to a big breakfast at Denny's, but didn't have to pay for it because someone on the other side of the restaurant gave my waiter a ten-spot and said, "It would be an honor and a blessing to buy that traveler's breakfast." I never spoke to, nor was I aware of that person, and after they fed me, they were gone.

On the road again, things seemed good. The morning was perfect riding weather, and Rosie was running smooth. My plan was to go from the Northwest corner of the state to the Southeast corner, about 450 miles. I was advised that the most direct route was under major construction, so I plotted a route through the mountainous country near Prescott.

At my first gas stop of the day, I met a fellow traveler. He introduced himself to me as "Yosushi Yoshimura–a Very Good Samurai Road Warrior." He was a long, long way from his home on Okinawa Island, Japan. When you are out on the road, it is easy to talk to other motorcyclists, because you are such a minority. My new friend was traveling from LA to New York City on a 650cc Suzuki Enduro, equipped with knobby, off-road tires. His only luggage was a duffel bungeed to the seat. He had purchased the bike in L.A. for 12,000 yen.

Yosushi's English was way better than my non-existent Japanese. He was very impressed with me and my bike. He knew that Rosie was a Nebraska-made Kawasaki by the rake of her handlebars. We had a nice talk, took pictures, exchanged addresses, blessed each other, and parted company. He was on his way north to see the Big Ditch and I was turning south. But for the rest of the journey, he was in my thoughts and prayers. I watched the Weather Channel each night with his route in mind as well as mine.

I headed off into the mountains to Prescott—way up, over, and down. Very scenic, lots of timber, curvy roads, and vistas. The angels and I had a nice worship time around Isaiah 40: "Make straight the highway....the valley shall be exalted, the crooked made straight, the rough places plain." I did make a few curves straight; it is hard to use only one lane when you are singing Handel's Messiah with a full orchestra.

It was a beautiful mid-day ride, but it slowed me down by an hour or two, and I had Phoenix and Tucson to get through. I wanted to avoid the rush hours, but it wasn't looking good.

When I came down off the mountain, it was clear that I was entering the real desert. It was 98 degrees hot in Phoenix and traffic was crawling. Now, as you know, sitting in stop-and-go freeway traffic is never fun. But sitting in stop-and-go traffic, while straddling a hot engine, in black leathers, with 98-degree sunshine on your plastic- encased head is pretty awful. At every chance, I started peeling layers. In Arizona, I never saw a biker with a helmet on, but I shed from the inside out, eventually losing everything except the exo-skeleton of my gear. I am fond of my skin and cranium.

When I stopped for gas in Chandler, the gas pump had a TV screen that talked to you and showed you commercials while you pumped. The sense that I was falling in and out of a time warp was intense, since 24 hours earlier I had hand-cranked a glass-vacuumed pump in Nevada. I was a bit homesick for those polite Oregon service guys. I come from one of the two states where it is illegal to pump your own gas. We are spoiled.

I decided to get off the freeway and wait out the traffic. I walked into a nice restaurant. I must have looked a little haggard. The waitress looked at me with concern, poured me a huge glass of water and then went back for the glass full of crayons. "Sit for a few minutes and relax, OK?" She seemed to think that coloring would help.

I tried to relax, and remarkably coloring a picture or two did make me feel better. After about a gallon of iced tea, I hit the road again. I stopped for the night at Wilcox, Arizona, about an hour after dark. I had made the ground I had set out to cover. But the heat had taken the starch out of me. Again, too tired to eat, I collapsed into a dreamless sleep.

Cats from the Freeway

In spite of a looming exhaustion that I could feel like a freight-train coming down the track, I woke at 5:50 am without an alarm. I had first coffee in the hotel with a couple of transplanted Northwesterners, who enjoyed chuckles with me over the fact that the locals were reporting an unusually wet and green spring. We agreed that they have no idea what green meant. But the desert in spring is an amazing thing. There are all kinds of wildflowers that you would never know were there at any other time. The cacti bloom in colors that Crayola has never mastered, even in their fluorescent collection. There are also clouds of seasonal bugs. These bugs eat lots of wild-colored pollen, and then they die violently on your windshield, leaving as their bequest amazing Jackson Pollock bug-death art. I had to stop every hour or so to wash away their contributions.

The plan for day five was to cover as much ground as day four. This meant scooting across the southern border of New Mexico and getting a good chunk of Texas behind me by nightfall. I had 850 miles to go and I wanted to knock off slightly more than half of that, stopping for the night at Fort Stockton, Texas. A wind had kicked up during the night, coming in straight from the east. A headwind negatively affects gas mileage. I prefer a tailwind, but either is preferable to strong cross-winds, which can affect handling.

The morning worship sharing centered on the One whose voice calmed both wind and wave. We sang, "It is Well With My Soul." The angels showed me a semi-trailer full of charity food and whispered, "You aren't the only crusader that we have out on this road." As I passed, the driver blew his horn and waved vigorously, for no reason that I understood.

All along the interstate in New Mexico, there are large white crosses painted on the pavement. They are there as navigation aids for small aircraft, but they pointed the way for me as well.

I stopped for lunch in Lordsburg, a barren little town by a train station that obviously shipped mostly cattle. I walked into a big cafe at the stockyards, empty except for three old ranchers sitting at the counter. The waitress turned around when I entered, and exclaimed,

"Lookie here boys, a road angel!"

(I looked over my shoulder.)

"You just sit anywhere you want, Angel."

We took a booth.

Mid-afternoon, near Deming, Rosie sputtered and choked. I had traveled 700 trouble-free miles, and had almost started to relax. I tensed instantaneously. The taste of sudden fear is not a taste that I have acquired—it is sour in the mouth and clenches the gut.

At this point, I started the rather bad habit of putting the bike in neutral, coasting along at great speed, then taking the key out of the ignition, opening the gas tank to vent the system, then returning the key to the ignition and re-starting the engine on the fly. Do not try this trick at home.

At the next chance, I pulled off the interstate at a truly abysmal Funky Gas. As soon as I stopped, several middle-aged guys jumped out of a van and engaged me. It turned out that they were the Les Filmore Blues Band from San Francisco, and they really wanted to sell me a CD. But the hard sell was called off when they realized that I was in distress about Rosie. They knew nada about bikes, but a lot about nurturing.

"Sweetie, this is OK—our van tries to break down all the time. Just baby her along and sing to her, and she'll get you there."

"Baby, you look tired—we could move the equipment around and try to roll that bike into the back of the van, give you a lift—That'd be OK, wouldn't it, Les? We're bound for San Antonio—Where y'all headed?"

Robert Frost was correct about the untaken road—you just never know. This was a real fork in the story. Who knows what would have happened if I had taken up with the blues band? I might have gotten to San Antonio a lot faster and learned a few tunes on the way.

I was sorely tempted to accept their offer. I was not worried about taking a ride from these strangers—they had that providential feel about them. They emanated safety. What tipped the scales was my sense of honor, or perhaps, foolish pride. I didn't want to take a lift. I had said I would ride, and ride I would. Anything else seemed like cheating. There would be no subway marathon for this Rosie! And so I declined their kind offer.

I do regret not buying a CD, but I don't really regret not taking the ride—I would have missed Adnan, Javiar, Luis and Rod (they are all coming up,) and a chance to learn a lesson about foolish pride.

Fortunately, Christ can see down all roads, and He doesn't abandon us when we pick a less promising one. I don't believe in finding "THE Right Choice" or "THE Choice that is His will." I believe that it is His will to travel with us, nothing else. If we consult our fellow traveler, He sometimes gives us good advice, but often He takes joy in the freedom of letting us choose and walking with us through our choices.

So I shared a Coke with those cats from the freeway, who composed a little "Motorcycle Blues" for me on the spot, and then they went on their way.

I got back on the road. Rosie was running OK, but not great. Topping the tank seemed to help. It put the problem at bay for 50 miles, but no more. I stopped at the next truck stop and bought a one-gallon plastic gas can, and used my bungee cords to affix it atop my pack behind my head. This allowed me to make very quick roadside stops to refuel my steed, and gave me back a hundred-mile range.

Back out on the road, I reassessed my plan for the day. It was clear that I wasn't going to make it to Fort Stockton. I decided that I would stop for some supper in El Paso, and then push on to Van Horn, a hundred miles closer.

I was halfway between Las Cruces, New Mexico, and El Paso when I started on the anti-pride curriculum. We were humming along when I observed that the gas gauge seemed to be falling rather quickly—as in, I could actually see the needle sinking steadily down towards 'E'. Mystified, I looked down at the engine, and saw a stream of gasoline spurting like an artery onto my left leg and the extremely hot engine.

This was not good. I pulled over. With the engine turned off, the leak slowed to a drip. I could see what had happened. The carburetor has a nice, crisp, square edge, and the fuel line had gotten kinked tightly over this edge. The vibration of the engine had, over time, allowed the carb to neatly saw through her own fuel line. My pristine brushed steel engine was black with burnt gasoline. I sat down on the bank of the road and let myself have a cry. It felt good.

Then I assessed my situation. Within a hundred yards of where I was stopped, there was a sign for the next exit, which promised a Super 8 Motel, the chain that was expecting me in Fort Stockton that evening. If I could get there, I could call ahead and cancel my reservation and make new plans. I got out the duct tape and wrapped the leaky line, then drove to the next exit.

Waiting for me at the motel was Adnan, a Pakistani MD starting over in Stateline, Texas. He called ahead for me while I tried to work on the bike. The tape had slowed but not stopped the leak. Dripping gasoline on a hot engine, even slowly, was just not an option. I tried cutting and re-clamping the line, but it was too short and wouldn't hold. Adnan informed me that in Pakistan, everyone is a motorcycle mechanic, and he seriously wanted to try and fix it with chewing gum, but I had had enough. Pride was jettisoned like granny's pump organ off the back of the covered wagon.

I called Mow Tow. It was 4 PM. A nice guy named Gary, who was ironically located in Las Vegas, Nevada, told me that I was only fifteen miles from El Paso and twenty from a motorcycle dealership. He would send a man named Javiar to pick me up, and call ahead to the dealer and ask them to wait for us. He said it would be one hour. I said "Thanks."

It turned out that Adnan was in the middle of studying for the psychiatric portion of the Texas Medical Boards, and was struggling with the differences between various mood disorders. Providentially for him, I had passed the National Counselor's Exam just six months previous and knew my mood disorders backwards and forwards. I spent the hour cheerfully tutoring him on depression and mania. This was especially easy because I was pretty much on a mood roller coaster.

At 5:10, Javiar and his helper Luis arrived in their pick-up truck. I was only a little disconcerted that "Javiar's Cycle Junk Yard" was painted on the side. Rosie was rolled up a ramp and secured in the truck bed. I was put in the middle of the bench seat up front between the guys. Javiar, about 50, was the friendly sort, and wanted the whole story. Luis, a lot younger, had little English, and I could tell from the look on his face that he had no Spanish words for me either.

As we crawled through El Paso's rush hour, Javiar apparently felt compelled to prepare me for the next stop.

"Now Peggy, This man Rod, (The shop owner)—He is not a bad man—but he has a very bad mouth. You are going to hear words that you have never heard before."

"Well, Javiar, I'll survive. If he's a good mechanic that will be enough..."

(Silence.)

"He is a good mechanic, isn't he, Javiar?"

"Weeeeell, he's OK. He closes at five, so probably he will just roll the bike in the back and work on it tomorrow. Ask to have his boy Mark work on her."

"Javiar, I have to be in San Antonio tomorrow."

"Hoo Boy! That's a funny one, Peg. Hey, Luis! Our preacher lady is funny."

We arrived at the dealership at 6:30. Rod was waiting with one mechanic, and Rod was not happy about it. I heard ten vulgarities and five profanities before I got out of the truck. He could swear verbally, adverbially, and in participle form. It was very impressive. Javiar marched up to Rod and straightened his small frame, and wagged his finger in Rod's face.

"Now you listen here, Rod. This lady is a classy lady, a preacher lady, a woman of God. She is on a Holy Journey. You treat her right–and you watch your mouth!"

Then Javiar took me aside and said, "I'm gonna leave now. Here's my pager number. I think Rod will behave, but if you need a ride to a hotel–Call Javiar, OK? Don't go nowhere with Rod."

Rod turned out to be OK. He had his boy Mark start on the fuel line, and listened to all my problems. I said that I had tried to cut and re-clamp the line. He said I should have used chewing gum. I could hear Pakistani chuckles from 20 miles away. He said Kaws cut their lines on a regular basis. He was sure that the stalling was a vacuum problem that would require taking the whole bike apart to find, but that it would be just a nuisance, not a big problem, and I should just ride with the gas cap open once I got to half a tank.

Rosie was ready to go at 7. Rod refused to write up the work, although he let me tip Mark. I rode off to find a room.

It had been a very long day, and I hadn't even made 300 miles. I was shaky tired. I had no enthusiasm, no joy, no awe left. Determination and confidence seemed to have been thrown off the wagon with pride. I knew that I would get up in the morning and move, but only because staying in El Paso was not an option. Too tired to eat or even shower, I slept. My brain tried to have a nightmare or two, but I was too tired to finish them.

Born To Be Mild

"Now, Faith is the certainty of things hoped for,
the proof of things that cannot be seen."

-Paul, to the Hebrews, 11:1, circa. A.D. 58

"Faith is what you either have or don't have left over when
Confidence, Joy, Awe, Pride and Determination
have all run out."

-Peggy, El Paso Texas, April 22, 1998

When I looked at the map the next morning, I discovered that I still had 548 miles to cross, through the width of the great state of Texas. I also discovered, in a back corner of my emptied-out heart, a small supply of faith. I cleaned up, found breakfast, and was on the road by eight.

The sky was clear, the wind was still mainly from the east and had whipped to a fury: 30 mph steady with 50 mph gusts. But the gusts never seemed to come straight on; they hit me from just to the right or the left. The interstate in Texas is a widely divided highway; I rode on the line between the two eastbound lanes, so that when the gusts knocked me sideways, I would still stay on the pavement. When the buffeting got dangerous-bad, I drastically decreased my speed to increase traction. But I really didn't have time to go slow.

The stretches of nothing between exits grew. The spare gas can came in handy. I filled it every chance I got. Rosie sputtered occasionally, but I was getting used to it, and let her have her gas cap open as soon as she was low enough not to splash when hitting potholes.

I topped one rise to find a valley full of dust devils; mini-cyclones, spinning around and kicking up dust and sagebrush. They didn't look too dangerous, and none of them were near the road, so I proceeded. At the bottom of the valley, one of them turned suddenly and seemed to race right at my right front side. It felt like being hit broadside by a truck. I was knocked to the left shoulder, and almost spun around. I was lucky to stay upright. I had to disentangle the bike and myself from a coating of tumbleweed.

I was starting to feel a little picked on. I registered my grievance with my Cosmic Tour Guide, loudly and with a bit of fist-shaking.

At that moment, a cry broke out above my head. I had seen birds all morning; lots of small hawks; and creepy, cartoon-true vultures that cruise the Texas roadsides for fresh road kill. But this cry was something else—it came from a larger bird of prey, circling barely 100 feet over my head. Its wingspan was at least three feet, and I could clearly see that its underside was light, except for the tips of its wings, which were the color of dried blood.

I stood, and listened as the bird cried out again, dipping and swooping towards me, before circling up and away. Her cry found an echo in the deepest regions of my soul, and I was aware of both the loneliness of the human soul in this Earthly Diaspora, and the immediate connection to the Source of all Life. The word that rose out of my resonating soul was Freedom. The freedom of God's very light touch —always present, never controlling—always providing, never preventing. This freedom is essentially tied in this world to a certain loneliness and a great deal of risk. I decided to accept this as my condition. I re-mounted and rode. I wasn't really anxious again on this ride.

That morning we sang an old family favorite:

He giveth more grace as our burdens grow greater.
He sendeth more strength as our labors increase.
To added afflictions He addeth His Mercy.

To multiplied trials, His multiplied peace.
His Love has no limit, His grace has no measure.
His Power has no boundary known unto men.
For out of His infinite riches in Jesus,
He giveth, and giveth, and giveth again.
When we have exhausted our store of endurance,
When our strength has failed ere the day is half done,
When we reach the end of our hoarded resources,
Our father's full giving is only begun."

("He Giveth More Grace" by Annie Flint & Hubert Mitchell)

I stopped that day for nothing else. I snacked at fuel stops. By mid-afternoon, my exhaustion and boredom were bordering on delirium. (I know that some of you think I was delirious long before this.) I started playing games with the angels to keep myself alert. After they beat me at travel bingo and an alphabet search, I decided that I was tired of traveling with unnamed companions and I announced that the next three proper names that I saw on signs would be their names, and invited them to help choose. Consequently, they became Cleophus (Cleo), Antonio (Tony), and Nelson. For some reason, at the time, this name search was the source of great hilarity.

Late in the day, the distances between towns began to shrink. I rode into San Antonio just as dark fell. It dawned on me for the first time that I had no idea where my hotel was actually located in this big city, except that it was on something called the Riverwalk. It was like finally making it to the Emerald City, and having no clue as to how to find the Wizard.

Mercifully, I soon saw signs for a "Riverwalk District." I ended up on Crockett Boulevard, in the middle of huge crowds. I started to be aware of barricades to the sides of the street, and then a city cop on a Harley Electra-Glide motioned me to the side. It turned out that the Holiness women had booked their convention in the middle of "Fiesta!", a week-long municipal bacchanalia, and I had nearly joined the opening night starlight parade. The nice officer gave me an alternate route to my hotel, and miraculously, I found it.

I parked in the circular drive of a rather nice, multi-story hotel. I shrugged my main pack over my shoulder and trudged my bow-legged, bug-encrusted, weary self, up to the registration desk. When the desk clerk acknowledged that, yes, indeed, I was expected, and had a bed waiting, a single tear of joy slid down my cheek. The desk boy tried to look sympathetic. He tried to help.

"That looks like a pretty heavy bag, can I carry it up to your room for you?"

"Sure," I replied gratefully, and plopped it in front of him.

"Man, this is heavy. Did you check it, or take it carry-on?"

(Not an amazingly observant boy, me in leathers with a helmet under my arm.)

"Uh... carry-on," I said.

"You're lucky you got it here. They're fussy about size these days."

"Oh, yes, I'm a lucky one."

I had a 7th floor corner room with a balcony. It came complete with amenities, including a blow-dryer, and I immediately thought about what I could have packed instead of my own, but decided I still needed the power tools for the road. Off my balcony, I could see and hear the parade.

I showered and changed, and because the dining room had closed for the day, I sat in the bar and ate a huge plate of truly excellent nachos with mesquite grilled chicken and real guacamole. (If you've ever eaten guacamole in the Southwest, you know the difference, if you haven't—there's no way to explain it.) I watched many Holiness-type women arrive, even some I knew, but they walked right past me. I was an unseen barfly, but a very grateful one. I ordered a celebratory Texas-sized margarita, and toasted the women, the angels, and the entire cloud of witnesses, with the toast of our Lord's Mother at the wedding of Cana, "Do whatever He tells you to do." (John 2:5)

Real Men Marry Preachers

The next day, I took a Thursday Sabbath. I slept until almost noon. Then, since it was too late to get breakfast in the hotel, I went walking up the Riverwalk, hoping for a bakery and good coffee.

San Antonio is an interesting city, and at the center of it is a below-street-level river, with walkways on either side. It is several miles long, garden-like in places, and lined with shops and eateries at other points. There are tour boats, ducks, and the occasional heron on the waterway. I even saw a couple of poisonous-looking water snakes; interesting at any rate.

I came upon a man sitting on a rock, reading. His T-shirt proclaimed "Real Men Marry Preachers." "John Stanley, I presume." said I, recognizing him as the husband of the convention organizer, and ex-professor of mine, The Reverend Doctor Susie Stanley. We had a nice chat, and he sent me in the direction of coffee and bagels. Later in the day, I bought one of those shirts.

Back at the hotel, I went to visit Rocinante in the stable. I borrowed rags and cleaning supplies from the housekeeping staff and soon had an audience of hotel employees begging stories. News apparently spread, because the next day, as I came back to my room, I overheard the two women making up my bed.

"It's true—she's one of those preacher women—but she rode a motorcycle all the way from Or-y-gone—see, there's her helmet."

"Where is Or-y-gone ?"

"I dunno. Up by Canada, I think."

"Sheesh—crazy preacher women!"

Some of you attentive readers may be wondering at this point why Rosie was not checked into the nearest Kawasaki dealership for a thorough check-up. I have no explanation for this, no excuse. I chalk it up to deep denial. For the moment I was safe, not moving for a few days, and I did not want to think about problems, mechanical or otherwise. I never gave a thought to the return ride, until it was time to leave.

After grooming the steed, I took a long nap and then ate dinner. By this time, I had found the rest of the ten women who made up the entire Quaker contingent among 400 clergywomen.

The meetings started after dinner. These were women from ten denominations, many countries and cultures, who shared a common call to ministry, and a common belief that a close connection to Christ will always translate into a transformed life. They were young, old, single, married, rainbow-colored and speaking with a polyphony of languages and accents, and all serious about their response to Christ.

The preaching, by some of the finest speakers on the planet, male and female, was phenomenal. But I experienced an odd reaction. I have experienced it before, but it was more acute this time. I often feel alone in a crowd, but oddly, the more "like me" the group is supposed to be, the lonelier I feel. I had a great deal in common with these women, but I felt most keenly, how different I was from them. How my call was to ride the fences of Christendom, neither exclusively tending the flocks and herds, nor seeking out the lost and wild. My call is to the margins. And it is to ride back and forth across the sometimes arbitrary lines we draw, reminding those on both sides of their similarities, not their differences.

I was also acutely aware that my friend and partner in crime and ministry, Alivia Biko, who was officially registered as my roommate, was 2200 miles away, too sick to attend. Ironically, I was less lonely, alone, out on the road. Here I was, the Lone Ranger, without Tonto, stuck in downtown Dodge with the townsfolk.

Davy Crockett: King of the Wild Frontier

Friday, after attending a good seminar on re-functioning dysfunctional churches, I went off to enjoy being a Fiesta tourista. To my great joy, I discovered that one of my carefully-laid plans had paid off. In the months before I left, I had meticulously broken in two pairs of Wrangler jeans, with just the right fit and extra leg length to create that nice cowboy scrunch, and I had my boots resoled rather than buy new ones. When you are in Texas, the last thing that you want to look like is a Yankee trying to look like a cowboy. To my delight, three people that afternoon, two of them Texans, asked me for directions. I passed.

I had business that day at the most sacred shrine in the Republic of Texas, The Alamo. (They are still pretty much in denial about the rest of the Union down there.) Back in Scotts Mills, there was a little boy named Garrett, age five at the time, who was a student of cowboy history, and a great admirer of Davy Crockett. Before I left, Garrett had approached me and said,

"Peggy, my mom says you are going to The Alamo."

"That's right, Garrett, I am."

"Are you taking a gun?" (On his videos the fight was still on.)

"No, Hon, I'm not planning to fight."

"Are you sure that's a good idea?"

"Yeah, I'm pretty sure the fighting is all over."

"OK, but be careful."

"I will."

It was my intention to get a photograph of myself on Rosie, outside of the traditional front door of The Alamo, holding a

Texas flag. I would then take the flag home to Garrett, to fly over his tree house.

When I got to the old mission in the middle of downtown San Antonio, I had to revise my plans. The front door that Crockett and company held against General Santa Ana was attended day and night by an honor guard. The entire grounds are treated as sacred. Wreaths are laid at the gates and in the building, perpetually replaced as they fade. Inside, no photos are taken, children are hushed, cowboys take off their hats, voices whisper. They take it all very, very seriously.

I got a motorcycle cop to take a photo of me and Rosie at a side gate on the street. I told him how far I had come to pay my respects, and he actually said, "Dang! That's a fur piece!"

I asked about pushing the bike, silently, reverently, up to the front gate for a portrait, and he said, "No Ma'am, that ain't allowed. I'd hafta take you in, and I'd hate to hafta take you in, comin' as fur as you did, an' all."

I did procure a flag and got a tourist to take a picture of me holding it at the front gate. Apparently, I held it wrong, because immediately at my side was an enormous Texan, who decided to teach me a little flag etiquette.

"Excuse me, ma'am, y'all need a little help, I see." He quickly took the flag from my hands and reversed it; maybe he was protecting me from imminent mob action. "You see, ma'am, the red goes below the white, because the blood of the martyrs had to come first to buy our freedom." Once again, freedom and its price were brought to my attention.

Doing It

Saturday morning, I presented my workshop on the prevention of family violence within Christian homes and churches. This flowed out of my work in Scotts Mills, after the murder of Laura Magee and her three preschool daughters. That church had commissioned me to take their concern for this situation to as many places as would hear me.

I spoke about the responsibility of the church to be at the forefront of the fight against violence. I made the case that living peaceably together in our homes is central to holy living. I spoke about the ways that the language, behavior and culture of Christendom can help, or hinder those seeking freedom from violence.

I gave my presentation twice that morning, and both sessions were well attended. I spoke to women who minister in churches, large and small; women who minister to teens and children. I put in their hands assessment tools and resources. And then I spent the afternoon doing what I always end up doing when I talk about this subject–talking individually with women for whom this is not an academic problem, or a ministry challenge, but for whom this is the daily reality of their lives.

I spoke to verbally abused, battered, and sexually abused wives, mothers, and ministers of God. Women who would lose their jobs if they told the truth. Women in ministry with husbands who preach Love and dispense hate in their homes. I gave them what hope and comfort I could. Just standing up and speaking about it brings them hope, or so they tell me again and again. I made suggestions to them about what actions they could take. I listened. But for many of them, the cost of speaking out seemed too great.

The church at large is still struggling with how to deal with this issue honestly, without punishing the people who bring it into the light. It was another long day; a productive, but heartbreaking day.

Having done what I came to do, I was ready to go home.

Our Lady of Junction

After some wild, wonderful preaching on Sunday morning, it was time to pack my bags and go. I pulled Rosie back into the elegant circular drive in front of the hotel for loading. Soon, I had collected a group of encouragers, most of them Holiness women. But a man and woman walked up, and seeing my Oregon license plate, introduced themselves as being residents of Mt. Angel, Oregon, where my friends the Benedictine sisters lived.

One vintage sister from Oklahoma asked if I could spare the time to give her a ride home. I told her that I had to preach next Sunday in Newberg, and she graciously let me off the hook. Good thing—laden as I was, I would have had to bungee the dear grandmother to my windshield.

A prayer circle was convened. The Mt. Angel couple stated, "We're Catholics, but we would like to pray for you too." They were made welcome. I knelt and was well blessed. Then, I lit outta there.

It had clouded over during the night, and just as I started to leave, a light rain began to fall. Well, actually it was nothing that any Northwesterner would call a rain, but the air did get damp. Ish. Just damp enough to raise six months of dust and oil on the road, but not damp enough to wash it away; "Slicker'n snake snot," as they say down there. So I slipped out of town, literally. But about the time I was ready to stop and get out my Gore-Tex rain suit, the sun came out, the road dried up, and I laid on the gas.

I stopped for lunch at a truck stop. The Texas-sized burger was great—they really do make everything huge down there—and the company was pleasant. The fellow next to me at the counter seemed to know a lot about bikes and asked me quite a few questions. But it seemed a bit odd that when I told him about the vacuum-locked valve, he looked a little sheepish. When I described the cut fuel line he looked embarrassed, maybe even something close to ashamed.

As a mental health professional, I am qualified to read emotional responses, and it looked to me like this guy felt personally responsible for my mechanical troubles. Mechanical codependency was a new one for me. So I asked him, "What is it that you do for a living?" He replied, "I'm the regional parts and sales manager for Kawasaki Motor Corporation—All those Vulcans do that, I'm awful sorry—but I'm glad our boys were out there in the desert when you needed them."

It's pretty hard to hold a grudge when the cosmos provides you with free mechanics and an apology.

Back on the road, the weather continued to improve, just as the weatherman had predicted—clear skies for the entire state by noon. At a town aptly named Junction, I stopped for gas. It was my plan to leave the interstate at this point and head due north on a main highway up to Abilene and then catch the next interstate west a few miles to Sweetwater, my goal for the night.

Junction has a quaint little gas station that features a Vend-O-Bait machine—convenience worms—another new concept for me. Sitting on the porch of this station was an old lady, nursing a soda in the afternoon sun. She watched me pump gas, she watched me pay for gas, and just as I was getting ready to leave she said:

"Where y'all goin'?"

"Up to Sweetwater via Abilene."

"Fixin' to take the highway?"

"Yes ma'am, straight north from here."

"Don't."

"Excuse me?"

"You don't want to go that way. You want to go up the back way through Eden and San Angelo."

"But my map shows the road through Abilene to be shorter."

"You deaf? (Pronounced deef) Or are you just not listening, girl? "

"Is there construction, or something I don't know about on the road to Abilene? "

"You're kinda' stubborn, ain'tcha? Or maybe you're just not a bright chile? You do as I tell you, ya hear?"

"Yes ma'am. Thank-you."

She just wasn't the kind of lady that you argued with and expected to win. Maybe I had gotten strange, but I decided to follow her advice to the letter. The roads she put me on were smaller, and longer, but all went well. About halfway north, I did notice some black storm clouds off to my right, but the sun shone on me the whole way.

At last, I pulled into Sweetwater and got my room. I turned the TV on in time to see a news report that Abilene had gotten hit by a freak thunderstorm that afternoon; they had six inches of rain, flash flooding, golf-ball sized hail and two tornado cells. All of this was directly on the route I had planned, and because of Our Lady of Junction, all precisely one Texas-sized county east of me.

Tucking Rosie in for the night, doing my normal stem to stern check, I noticed that the fuel line was attempting to open up again. I looked in the local Yellow Pages and found one motorcycle establishment, Sweetwater Cycle—a Harley Dealership. Asking a Harley mechanic to work on your "Rice Burner" (translation: Japanese bike) often gets you the same reaction you would get asking a French waiter for catsup for your foie gras. And this American establishment was not scheduled to open 'til Tuesday.

I called the listed number anyway. It rang at the home of the owner, Jason, who listened to my story, and agreed to meet me at his shop the next day at 9 am after he got his kids off to school. He made sure that I was carrying metric tools, informing me that his shop was strictly American socket stocked. Grateful, I slept.

I Heard the Approach of Four Horsemen

When I awoke in Sweetwater that Monday morning, I discovered that during the night my heart had caught up with my body and turned the corner towards home. It is always a risky thing to fly faster than your heart, but sometimes a body just can't help it. Home now seemed reachable, and it called to me. Just then, my head caught up with my body and my heart, and reminded me that I had a sermon to write.

Since I needed to wait a couple of hours for Jason to get his kids off to school, I decided to have a nice long breakfast and work on my message. The motel had a pleasant café, so I tucked in to what passes ` for a "continental" breakfast in Texas: ham steaks, eggs, potatoes and pancakes, washed down with fresh squeezed juice, milk, and a gallon or two of coffee.

I also settled into my writing. My assignment was the Apocalypse of John, especially the topics of war, rumors of war, and the "War of the Lamb." My goal was to make it clear that this last message from the last apostle was a message of hope. It is one of the greatest of the pert near true tales. It tells about a future where Christ himself wages war against evil, hate and death—where Truth is victorious.

I was in the middle of pancakes and apocalypse when a lovely woman came across the dining room to my table.

"Excuse me—I hate to interrupt your breakfast, but I was wondering if you are a horsewoman."

"No, Not really, why do you ask?"

"I couldn't help but notice your leather britches. I assumed you were riding. "

"Well, I am, but my horse is a Kawasaki motorcycle."

"I see." (long pause) "Well, you may think this is very odd, but I was sitting across the room and felt very clearly led to come over and give you this."

And she handed me a postcard with a painting of the Four Horsemen of the Apocalypse on it. I sat in stunned silence. Eventually she continued.

"I'm so sorry, I'll let you finish your meal."

"No, really, I'm just a little surprised, you see I am sitting here writing a sermon about this very text—please, sit down and have breakfast with me."

She did. I discovered that I was talking to Dr. Marilyn Todd-Daniels, a Methodist minister who was traveling to bring the Gospel to people through the arts. We had a nice, long talk about being women in ministry on the road, about art, about my sermon, about horses, and many other things.

When breakfast was gone, she gave me another card, this one with a picture of Christ on it, and a text from Paul's chat at the people in Phillipi, Greece. She said, "I think you should give this to that pastor back in Oregon where you are going to preach Sunday." I tucked it in my Bible. Marilyn accompanied me back to my room, and prayed a blessing upon me and my steed, and then we "left out," as they say down there, to find Jason.

Sweetwater Cycle was a large old garage and shop. Jason, and his youngest, Hayden, age two, were there to help me. Jason hardly complained at all about the metric requirements. He didn't even criticize the previous repairs too badly. He did send me over to NAPA for some metal clamps to replace the plastic ones.

Apparently, they don't see many women in leathers in the auto parts store in Sweetwater. There were three guys in ball caps and one fellow behind the counter when I walked in, yakking away till they saw me. Could've heard a ball bearing drop. I was immediately at the head of the line, and the center of attention. Eight eyeballs were glued to me. I said the magic words, "Jason sent me over for some hose clamps," and suddenly I was family. I paid 25 cents for the parts.

Jason replaced my wimpy Japanese fuel line with a big honkin' hunk of Harley hose. Being a genius, he then took another hunk of fuel line and split it and wedged it between the line and the carb. Then, being a thorough genius, he gave me another hunk for my kit. "When the wedge begins to wear, replace it with this one, then the line itself will never be compromised." It was so obvious—afterwards.

Jason's repair lasted all the way home, and has not worn through to this day. He was the last mechanic that I talked to on this trip. But again, he took no money from me, so I blessed his baby, and headed north about 11 AM. I rode off, thinking pretty heavily about the walls that we build between each other over things as arbitrary as where your bike was assembled. It occurred to me that the only thing needed to breach those walls was willingness. You start with the willingness to lay down your own tools, to invite someone into your space and bring your skills and their tools together to help someone who needs it. It seems so obvious—afterwards.

My goal for the day had been Santa Fe, New Mexico, and if I had left before breakfast, I would have made it. But there was not anywhere near enough time for that now, so I just pointed her at the New Mexico border and let her fly.

Mid-afternoon, I hit a cold front coming in from the west. The temperature dropped from 58 to 40 in an hour. And the east winds that had blown in my face heading towards Texas now turned, and blew hard from the Northwest; hard and cold, and in my face again. I passed through Lubbock and crossed the border at Clovis around three o'clock. I then gained an hour for the good sense of being westbound. I was half frozen by the time I reached Fort Sumner around suppertime. The temperature had continued to drop, and the wind speed had risen until they were both in the mid-thirties. I got a room with a view of the graveyard where they buried Billy the Kid. I asked the angels to watch my back while I slept. They obliged.

The Land of Enchantment

I rose early, Tuesday, said a prayer for the soul of Billy and young sociopaths everywhere, and headed north. It was still cold and I put on every layer of clothing that I could. I stopped for breakfast at Santa Rosa. I ate and conversed with a Hispanic trucker named Hector, who started the conversation like this.

"You out on the road?"

"Yep."

"Alone?"

"Yeah, ...mostly."

"I used to be a Disciple." (This caught my attention.)

"Excuse me?"

"Yeah, I rode with the Disciples back east."

"Oh..." (I got it now, the motorcycle gang called The Disciples.)

"When I came out to L.A., I rode with "The Chosen Few."

"Well, it's nice to have friends," I said, stretching for a polite response.

"Sure is," said Hector with deep feeling.

We talked about the weather (he said I was heading towards snow) and my trip. He told me some funny stories about riding in a motorcycle club to illustrate how we bikers are so misunderstood by citizens (that's the rest of you.) My favorite one was about the time that 50 or so of the Few came across an elderly couple in a big old Buick, stopped out in the middle of nowhere, on a hot day, with a flat tire. Being Good Samaritans, the bikers pulled over en masse and offered to assist the couple who, oddly, (to the biker's thinking), locked their doors and wouldn't get out of the car.

The bikers got the spare out of the trunk, (he didn't say how they got into the trunk), but apparently the citizens had no tire jack. "What kind of crazy people travel without a jack?" commented Hector. So a dozen or so of the Chosen Few gathered around the back of the car and lifted it off the ground, elderly couple still inside, while Hector and another man changed the tire. He said that the couple did manage to wave a weak "thank-you" as the bikers rode off. The moral of the story, according to Hector, was that "Some folks don't know angels when they see them."

Then Hector cracked up. "Hey, I made a joke. We weren't Angels, we were The Chosen!"

This Hell's Angels joke was getting old, but the boys and I laughed loud and hearty anyway. Then we hit the road. Before I made it far on Interstate 40 going west, I started to see snow on the sides of the road, but the day was sunny and it was warming fast.

When I made Cline's Corners, 60 miles east of Albuquerque, they told me that the whole area had been hit by a freak snowstorm the day before. They had 12 inches of snow in an area that usually gets one or two dustings a year, and that in the dead of winter, never this late in the Spring. The interstate had been closed for 12 hours overnight and a large contingent of bikers coming out of Nevada (probably from the very same gathering that I missed in Fallon) had been stranded overnight. One biker had been airlifted out of this very truck stop with a severely broken leg that he got dumping his bike on the exit ramp. I took a few deep breaths. If it hadn't been for my delay in Sweetwater, I would have been right in the middle of it.

But the road continued to be clear and dry for me. As soon as I left 'The Corners', as they call that spot, I had the refreshing, comforting sensation of being on roads that I knew well from my college days at St. John's in Santa Fe. I poured on the gas, because I knew that if I could get into Santa Fe before two o'clock, I could feast on the best food in the hemisphere: blue corn/green chili tacos at The Shed, my favorite Santa Fe restaurant. They only serve lunch, so I had to scoot. I planned to go no farther that day.

The town had sprawled a bit in 20 years, but the downtown was remarkably unchanged from my student days, or for that matter from the days of the conquistadores. I guess that shouldn't have surprised me, as much of it has been standing since the 1500's. Santa Fe was a bustling town when Plymouth Rock was just a rock.

I pulled into my destination, La Posada, just after noon. 'La Po' as we always called it, is a couple blocks off the Plaza, and the most sophisticated resting place in town. As students, we saved up our money to have an occasional drink in the elegant bar. Eating in the dining room was not an option unless somebody's rich parents were visiting. But I had promised myself that if I ever came back, I was going to have the best, and I did; a little adobe three-room suite complete with a kiva fireplace, and a boy who came at your call to light the fire. I was checked in and downtown eating blue corn by 1:30.

The rest of the afternoon was spent shopping, the primary activity of the region. I was specializing in tiny presents for the folks back home. I also walked unannounced into the law office of an old schoolmate. I enjoyed watching his brain gears strip as he went through –wait– I know you—Peggy. I was severely out of time and context. I left with a date for dinner.

I then paid a visit to one of my favorite spots, Loretto Chapel. This miniature cathedral is most famous for its "Miraculous Staircase," made, as the locals tell it, by a mysterious carpenter named José (Joseph, yes, that carpenter!)

The story goes that the Sisters of Loretto had their chapel built as a miniature reproduction of a certain European church, but it became clear that scaled-down stairs to the choir loft were not going to be functional. A normal sized staircase would have taken up half of the chapel floor space. The sisters resigned themselves to having a useless loft. Then one day, a man walked in, leading a burro loaded with wood—a traveling carpenter who had heard of their problem. He offered to build them a spiral staircase. He worked quietly, and quickly. He built a most amazing set of stairs that curls upward in a perfect spiral without any support posts whatsoever. He left without taking any pay, giving only the name of Jose. (Does this not sound like a few mechanics we have met?) That staircase stands today, polished by the quiet feet of religious women, hundreds of years later.

I like the place, even though it is now a tourist attraction. It has retained its quiet and beauty, and it feels unusually holy to me. That afternoon, I decided to ignore all the tourists and kneel at the altar to pray. I stayed for quite a while, because my Lord and I were having such a nice chat.

On my way out, I stopped in the gift shop, and on an impulse, bought myself an amethyst and silver rosary. The man running the place said, "I sure am glad you came here today, Peggy." (Pulling my name off my credit card) "Did you ask for everything you really wanted?"

"No" I said, suddenly realizing that a deep desire of mine had gone unspoken. So I went back to the chapel altar and not knowing how to say a rosary correctly, I just stated my desire, in as many ways as I could, and alternated it with thanks until I ran out of beads.

"How come Alivia isn't OK?" I asked again and again, and then waited.

Then He answered, "She looks just fine to me."

"You know what I mean." I hate smart-aleck Jesus.

"What would you have me do?"

"I want her strong, and healthy, and as physically free as she is spiritually free."

"Sometimes I require an instrument for this type of work. Are you willing?"

"No problemo... Yes."

"It will be the most expensive thing you have ever done. Restoring life requires great Love and great sacrifice. Are you really ready to sign a blank check?"

"Hand me the pen."

Then I left again. The shopman waved me out, saying, "Miracles still happen, you know; and you look like the kinda gal who still believes. Ride safe!"

Outside, I was just in time to see one of the four pm thunderstorms for which Santa Fe is famous. Then I had a good dinner, a visit to the old alma mater, and a good sleep.

Rocky Mountain High

It was 28 degrees when I woke up. I waited until it warmed to 32, then I knocked the frost off Rosie and bid Santa Fe a fond farewell. A decision needed to be made at this point: to go back down south to Albuquerque and take the interstate west, or to go north and higher into the mountains. The western route would eventually take me back through Nevada, an abhorrent idea. But the northern route required the crossing of a bit of Colorado, and a little bit of the Rockies in the form of the 8,000-foot Mancos Pass. Having no snow tires or chains in my pack, it was a crucial decision, but the sun was shining, and I decided to believe the sun. I left Santa Fe to the north.

There really is no place on the planet like northern New Mexico for naked beauty. The ride was fabulous—curvy, on sparsely trafficked roads. Tall mountains form the backdrop for canyons, and lakes, and forests. We sang all the way. Worship sharing commenced again. I was just about to ask the boys what they had to show me, when we reached what I presume was the New Mexico state line. The only marker was a sign that read "Vaya Con Dios" (Go with God.) I accepted this as their contribution.

The road rose every hour. I had lunch in Pagosa Springs, Colorado, and it was nice enough to eat outside at a picnic table. An hour later, I was through the old silver mining town of Durango, altitude 6500 feet. An hour after that, I was approaching the pass—another 1000 feet up.

The temperature had been dropping, and the sky clouded up. A very cold rain started to fall. It was 38 degrees and raining at the top of the pass. On the bike, wind chill dropped that quite a bit. The road got slick. The altitude was extreme enough that Rosie started to wheeze a bit from lack of oxygen to mix with her gas. I stopped to tweak the mixture and actually wrung the water out of my electrically heated gloves. I plugged them back into the 12-volt power connection, and put them back on. When they heated back up, steam rose from them. I knew if they shorted, I would be in for a serious shock, but without them I would not be able to feel my hands or control the bike.

For the next hour, I was steam-baking my hands while the rest of me froze. Hell frozen over. Baked Colorado. There was not a habitation to shelter me. I knew I had ancestors from these parts. I was only a couple of counties away from the spot where my dad's grandpa froze to death on his motorcycle. Guess he didn't have a horse. Horses are warm. I wondered if he was watching me. I wondered if I would be joining him soon.

Finally, the road turned down towards the town of Cortez. I stopped in a wide spot, turned around and looked back at the edge of the Rockies. The sun came out like it had never been gone, the road was dry, and the clouds were massed behind those peaks like Einstein on an especially bad hair day. I was grateful that I had only seen a little of those mountains. I switched out my wet gloves for non-heated but dry ones and a white, peeling layer of skin-gloves came off with them. I proceeded with lobster hands.

I was tired, but it was only three o'clock, so I pressed on. That part of southern Utah is nothing to write home about, except the area around Moab. Here, God has hidden some great sculpture. Mesas and arches, canyons and gorges, all carved over the millennia into rock so red, you swear it can't be real. The sky is a color of blue that I have only seen elsewhere in a box of crayons. I arrived in this bit of Mars on Earth just as the sun was getting low. A tour guide couldn't have planned it better.

I made it to Green River, Utah, Wednesday night, a little past sunset. I had bested 500 miles once again. I have no conscious recollection of where I stayed that night. I was slipping well into zombie mode.

Driving like Jehu

The watchman shouted to the King, "The messenger has arrived, but he isn't coming back! He must have found Jehu son of Nimshi, for he's driving like a madman."

-II Kings 9:20

The rest of this story is going to go pretty much like the rest of the ride. It was a bit of a blur. I came down with a bad case of nose to the barn syndrome. Home-focused tunnel vision.

It was Thursday morning, the last day of April. I was 1,100 miles from home, and I was determined to eat dinner in my own house, with my own family, on Friday evening. The rest of the way, I talked to very few people; I hardly ate. I fueled and snacked at rest areas. But at one of Utah's immaculately clean rest stops, I broke out of my trance and had a familiar chat with a small female human.

She was wearing a blue cotton dress; her neat braids were thick and yellow. She was waiting outside a restroom with a group of genetically similar siblings. The big brother assigned to watch her was looking at other things. The small girl's attention was captured by the motorcycle rider that pulled up. Her eyes got very big when the rider took her helmet off and smiled at her.

"Hey, pint-size."

The girl mustered up her six years of courage and spoke to the stranger from another planet.

"Hello, um, are you a lady?"

"Yes, I am a lady." I said.

"I didn't know ladies could have motorcycles!"

I looked about, leaned forward, and whispered to the child in my best conspiratorial voice,

"Sure, they can. You just have to wait until you are big enough. But don't ask beforehand–just do it–it's always easier to get forgiveness than permission."

The little girl's eyes turned to saucers as a big sister came out of the ladies room, swooped her up and put her into the back of a van. The little one never took her eyes off me, clearly thinking shiny new thoughts in her little head as they drove away.

This vignette never gets old.

If I had more time with the little ones, I would explain the difference between blessing and permission. I would explain how I came to discover that the desire for a blessing can be life-giving to a relationship, and how the need for permission can be poisonous. But I have settled for planting little seeds of subversive freedom in their heads and hearts, and I trust my good and loving God to teach them the rest of the lesson in due time.

On my way again, I was slowed by heavy construction in Salt Lake City at about noon, but I still made Boise, Idaho, by nightfall. Just to keep my thermostat confused, it was getting hot again. Rush hour traffic in Boise was as bad as Phoenix, only 80 degrees rather than 98. I slept in a motel I don't remember, somewhere on the west side of Boise.

Friday morning, I needed to decide whether to bisect Oregon from Ontario to Bend, or come down the Columbia Gorge. The Bend way was shorter and avoided Portland rush hour, but would make the Cascades my last challenge. I had my last clear direction from the boys when I looked at the map, and felt a big, "No - No - No" when I looked at the back roads of eastern Oregon. I took the Gorge. I will never know what it was I missed on the other route, but I really don't care. I'm just glad I missed it.

When I crossed the Oregon border, I stood up on my pegs, punched my left fist in the air, and let out a rebel yell that would have made Davy Crockett proud. When I next got off for fuel, I had been pumping my own gas for so long that I was startled when the man came up to me and said "Whoa there, this is Oregon, you can't run the pump for yourself."

Tears came to my eyes; I kissed the attendant on the cheek, and went inside and ordered a piece of Marion berry pie and a latte. Home. Sigh.

When I got gas next at Hood River, I was grinning. The boy said, "What's got you so happy? "

"I'm almost home."

"Where's home? "

"Salem."

"You aren't anywhere close to Salem, lady."

"Son, I am a lot closer to Salem than I am to Texas."

When I got to Portland, I discovered that the whole state had been having an early May heat wave. Rush hour was bad, so I got off the gridlocked Banfield Freeway and onto surface streets. Desperate to look into the eyes of someone who knew me, I headed for Alivia's house. No luck, she was on her way home from Seattle that day, and I had beat her from Boise. I ran by my friend Marge Abbott's house, but she also was not home. Her husband Carl was home, however, and by the look in his eyes, I could tell that I must have looked pretty ragged. Just because I was 15 pounds lighter, burned in some places and deadly pale in others, dirty from head to foot, and encrusted in dead insects; this was no reason to shun me, so Carl asked me in and offered me a cup of cold water. A righteous man.

I took off and was home in Salem by six pm. The dog heard me first, I am told, and started jumping at the door. I rolled in, just in time for supper. My place at the table was set. The people around the table had become suddenly beautiful, and smart, and kind. The food the kids were turning their noses up at was gourmet, my tub was a spa. My bed was heaven.

I slept most of Saturday. Sunday morning broke beautiful, balmy and sunny. I arrived in Newberg via my car, in a dress, with time to spare before the first service. Pastor Dick Sartwell beamed at me. Alice Maurer, home from the conference a week ahead of me, looked relieved to see me.

In the middle of the first service, Dick read a scripture that he had prepared, not knowing precisely what verses I was going to use for the sermon. He read from Paul's letter to the Philippians, Chapter 2; which took me right back to Sweetwater. I looked in my Bible, and there was the card given to me by the artist, the very same verse. I gave it to him, as she had instructed.

I preached all three services with energy, joy and power. I preached the Revelation of John. I spoke about Honor, and Valor, and Sacrifice. I spoke about how we have nothing to fear from a God who knows us, watches us, and gives his angels to care over us. I told them about a God who has prepared the road ahead of us. A road that may have its share of dangers, but a road that is studded with the miraculous.

I had never before experienced such a feeling of deep congruence. Things that I had previously believed, I now KNEW, and I knew I would never be able to entertain doubt about His goodness afterwards. I was a witness to His works. I had seen them with my own eyes; I had heard them with my own ears.

I am a witness. I am an Apostle.

Part 4:
Says Who?

So what does Odysseus do when he has been tried, tested, and returned to his Penelope? Well, at first, he goes all Dorothy and swears never to go any farther than his own back yard. This lasts for a month or two. He tells a lot of tales, but his friends eventually get tired of them. After a while, Penny gets fed up with his moping about and suggests that he get out of her hair for a bit. He decides to take the boat out for a little fishing. It is only supposed to be for an afternoon…

Bucephalus

I tried polyamory for a while. Rocinante's fuel limitations got me looking at long haul bikes. The dream bike of this genre is the PD1000—PD standing for Paris to Dakar. I had been having a recurring dream about Africa for a while—something about Dakar called to me. Fortunately, I had the God-given sense to not trade in Rocinante. My friend Owen does not name his bikes. He says it makes it too hard when it comes time to put them down. He is right. Rosie has been with me too long and I have so thoroughly anthropomorphized her that after I am gone, one of my progeny is going to have to work up the courage to do something with her. But I started to think that it would be okay to add another steed to the stable.

I went back to Taylor Honda and talked about long rides. I found out that Beemer had stopped making the PD, so I was looking at anything with a big gas tank. Kawasaki made a street version of their police bike called the Concourse, or ZG1000—800 lbs., 1000 cubic centimeters. Old man Taylor had a pretty blue one. By this time, I had a steady caseload of trauma clients and some spending money of my own. I took it home.

I named it Asfoloth Bucephalus, after an elven horse and Alexander's ride, and it defied the rule of ship and sea by not seeming very female. I took off the Kaw badges and slapped on decal kanji that I was told said Truth and Power—of course it might have said STUPID and AMERCIAN for all I know of kanji, but I thought it looked pretty cool. Astride it, I could put my feet flat, but just barely. The tank held seven gallons—almost 300 miles.

But the tank was way up high and that made the whole business very top heavy.

I was going about 95. That was a bit supra-legal, but it was on an empty, straight, flat piece of road on a clear, dry day in the middle of a county that has a population of about one person for every ten square miles—so—a speed appropriate for the conditions.

AB was big and new and it was not using half of the RPM's it had available. My back was not used to the forward lean of the sport-bike seating configuration, so I would occasionally take one hand off the controls and twist my arm behind me to stretch out the kinks.

Taking your left hand off the controls of the bike has no effect. That hand is holding the clutch, and unless you are in the process of shifting, you can let go. The right hand is on the throttle, so unless your bike is equipped with some sort of cruise control, when you let go with the right hand, you start to slow down. But for the length of a stretch, that is fine. Your right foot has a brake and your left foot has the gearshift. Control is diversified—a good idea, whatever your endeavor.

It was during a round of this back stretching, including twisting in the seat and shifting my weight all around that I came to realize a thing about my new bike. It is incredibly stable at speed. It just hums along, rock solid, until you give it a clear and undeniable instruction.

That is when the idea occurred to me: what happens if you take both hands off the bike at the same time? In grade school I used to ride my Schwinn 'no hands' all the time. Would it be the same?

Impulse control has never been my deepest suit.

I covered both handles and then just loosened my grip incrementally until my hands were hovering above but not touching the handlebars—no change, except for the slow deceleration—nothing, nada. I gave it more gas and then let go again, this time putting my hands in my lap—like a train on rails. Gas again, and release, and then I pushed a bit with one knee and then the other. I could steer a bit this way, but mostly it just tore on like a bullet. Until I let the deceleration progress too far. Instability started to creep back in at about 60. I gave it all four appendages again, exhilarated and thoughtful.

Stability increases with speed. This is true for motorcycles. You are much more likely to drop your bike rolling it around a parking lot than you are at highway speeds. This is physics ala Brother Newton. It is called inertia–rule number one–moving things want to move, sitting things want to sit. On a bike, go fast and inertia is your friend, speeding you along in a straight line. In a parking lot, inertia will gladly scratch up your paint, as your bike attempts to stay at rest. Of course, going too fast, inertia can cause personal aviation, especially if for any reason you forsake traction.

I am grateful for my riding experiences. I never fail to find spiritual application from the mindfulness that a bike requires of you. I have decided that I believe in the principle of Spiritual Inertia.

I have written about the need to sometimes slow down, way down, emotionally and spiritually in Retreat. You have to fight the inertia of busyness to do it. But you reap rewards from it.

Yet, sometimes, positive inertia can be your friend.

When I am feeling emotionally and spiritually unstable, if rest doesn't fix it, then I probably need to give the engine some gas and get moving. Fight the inertia that would keep me stuck. I need to do the things in front of me; invest, engage, proceed. Sometimes, I just need to trust the forward motion of my life to carry me across the occasional pothole to a better road on the other side.

Probably might as well hang on, though.

The Scariest Day

The scariest day of my life included no physical danger to me. I wasn't seeking out any unusual risks. I was in complete denial about the usual risks. The biggest risk any of us take on a regular basis is letting someone we love out of our sights. When you love, you greatly broaden your risk horizon. Anything that happens to your beloved has the power to hurt you. Anyone you love has been given an all-access pass to your heart; betrayal or loss can roll through your soul like a hurricane, flattening everything in its path.

The greatest of these love-risks is to be a parent. There is no love so instantaneous or deep. If you know what is good for you, you understand that you have to start letting go of them by millimeters from the beginning. Because the only other choice is to try and build walls around them and keep them under watch. And love, by its very nature, precludes the taking of prisoners.

The greatest lovers in the world are also the greatest gamblers.

I was sitting in my office at 10 am on a Thursday morning when the phone rang.

"Hello? Peggy? You don't know me; I am the mother of your daughter's boyfriend. He brought her to the hospital last night. She has a bad case of influenza. She's having trouble breathing. They want to intubate her, and she is refusing, and no one here can over-rule her. I am so sorry, but I think you had better get on a plane."

Emily was 20. She was a student at the University of New Mexico in Albuquerque. I knew the guy in her life. He seemed solid and she seemed happy. They had recently gotten an apartment. That turned out to be a good thing, because he was there when the flu went respiratory and her asthma kicked in. She didn't want to go to the ER. He made her—pretty much picked her up and carried her, and she was too sick to fight. I will always love him for that.

I called her father at work, threw some things in a bag, ran down the stairs and gave the situation to my old dad. I jumped in the car and started the hour's drive to the airport. Dad was on the phone with the airline, begging them to get me on the only non-stop of the day. He succeeded. When I got to the airport, pre TSA—thank God—they were expecting me. I actually made it to the gate with 20 minutes to spare.

I had no cell phone. No way to check on her, I just had to get there as fast as I could. The spare minutes were not actually welcome. I was good as long as I was moving. As soon as I had a moment to wait, I about came to pieces. I do not like to cry in public. I consider it to be unseemly. I told Jesus that I needed a real good human to pray for me, and I needed one now.

I looked up and saw a Friend walking towards me. Mr. Bill Joliff. A Quaker, a bluegrass musician, and a very close friend of my friend Jesus. Bill took a look at me and asked what was wrong. He set right in to prayin'. He prayed me onto the plane. On the plane he was replaced by an old lady seatmate who had her Bible out and ready to go. I made Albuquerque by 4pm and the hospital by 5.

My daughter's young man was upset. It was clear he loved her and his risk meter was in the red zone. His mother wasn't far behind, as what risked my daughter risked her child, which risked her own heart. What a chain of fear it was.

They had Em on the cardiac intensive care floor—I did not like that. The doctor was waiting for me. She said that my firstborn was not getting enough oxygen. Intubation was required, but my 98 lb., strong-willed, scrapper of a daughter was refusing, clearly and regularly. Everyone had tried to reason with her. Everyone had failed. The doc admitted to giving her morphine, in hopes that she would conk out and they could do what they wanted, in her best interest. Emily refused to shut her eyes.

The doctor and I walked in. Emily looked tiny under the sheet, her skin had a bluish cast. That girl, who had called me "Mother" since she was a precociously adult six year old, took one look at me and whimpered "Mommy!" like a toddler. The doc pulled up the bottom of the sheet to show me that her toes were purple. She had been a lavender-blue baby the day she was born. It wasn't a good color for her, ever.

I told the doctor to give us five minutes alone.

I crawled up into the bed with her. I told her that she wasn't alone and that I would watch over her. She took one deep breath and settled onto my shoulder and succumbed to sleep. I set in to prayin'. The doc came in with a cart of equipment and a nurse.

I said, "She has relaxed and is breathing deep—can we give her five more minutes?"

Her color was improving. The doc stayed. I prayed and breathed with her.

"Five minutes up," said the doc. "Really, this is going to help her."

"Check her toes."

They were pink. "I'll be..." said the doc. "Are you all this stubborn?"

"Pretty much."

They never intubated her.

Because what love risks, sometimes, love can heal.

The Missionary Position

My mother wanted me to marry a pastor. I became one instead. She would have been okay with that, if she had lived to see it. Holiness mothers have to be okay with any of the traditional God-callings, even for girls. My mother was known to preach now and then. Holiness mothers of my mother's vintage lived in fear of God calling one of their children to the mission field—because they would have to be okay with that. But truthfully, the last thing they wanted was for their grandbabies to be off in some dangerous place full of snakes. I had her grandbabies in Oregon, which was too far away and too backwards for her tastes, but she could get to us by phone or plane or train, and the snakes aren't too bad.

In the spring of 2002, I was busy being a trauma healer and occasionally being an itinerant preacher and family violence preventer. Alivia Biko had settled into my world as a co-worker and friend. She sang and I preached and we called it "Sister Love's Traveling Salvation Show," as a joke that mitigated our horror at having clearly become evangelists. I thought that was a bad as it could get.

Then the African arrived. His name is David Niyonzima. He is a Quaker. That spring, he was studying to become one of the handful of trauma healers in the Central African nation of Burundi. The entire country had been specializing in ethnic trauma for a couple of generations, with the usual catastrophic results.

I was editing a book on Quaker ministry. He had written an essay for said book, and I was picking it up. He seemed like a charming fellow, and I liked him immediately. While we were talking, I had a bit of a God moment, a clear but quiet voice ringing up from down inside me someplace.

As a mental health professional, these moments are a bit disturbing. I stake my tentative sanity on the knowledge that the voice was inside me. The debatable bit, sanity-wise, was the certain knowledge that the voice was not mine. The technical term for this belief is thought-insertion. It can be a symptom of schizophrenia. If you hear the voice and believe it to be external, that is an auditory hallucination—also sometimes a symptom of schizophrenia. Fortunately, an occasional symptom or two, a disorder does not make. Quakers call this voice The Present Christ. It's okay with me if you think we are delusional.

So the Voice said, "Do whatever this man asks of you."

And right after that, Niyonzima said, "Peggy, I know we have just met, but I have a big favor to ask of you." His problem was that eight weeks before picking up his master's degree, he found out that he had a requirement for 12 weeks of personal psychotherapy. They gave him a list of professionals who all got top dollar. This man had only francs and not many of those. I had the right professional creds. He asked me to see him twice a week, pro bono. I said yes.

Not much else was ever the same.

He also admitted that he was going back to heal a nation of 7 million trauma victims and the program had trained him to be an American psychotherapist and had not given him one single course in trauma healing. I was on speaking terms with the best traumatologist in the nation and had just taken his intensive course.

I saw Niyonzima three times a week, for eight weeks, for therapy and instruction. And at the end he said,

"When are you coming?"

"Coming?"

"To Burundi—I need your help."

I said yes. It took me a year to arrange, but in 2003, I left for the first of three longish trips to Central Africa.

Just before I left, my father was diagnosed with bladder cancer. I almost cancelled the trip. Neither of my brothers wanted me to go. I let my dad make the final determination. We were very close. I was not my mother, but I was as close as he had to that kind of support.

He said, "Your mother and I raised you for this. It would be selfish of me to keep you. God knows our needs. Do whatever He tells you to do." And he gave me another set of wings.

Alivia moved in and took care of my dad in my stead, and I followed that call.

Powerless

I arrived in Central Africa unprepared. There isn't really any other way to go. But it was actually my first trip outside of North America, on my first trip to what is called the Third World. It's a long trip. There is no direct route to Burundi. This is probably a good thing because the case of the cultural bends that you get, even with several stops, is bad enough.

I was traveling alone, and it did not take long for me to realize that my personal power meter was dropping precipitously as I proceeded. Seattle—not home. Amsterdam—losing language and culture skills. Nairobi, Kenya—things start to get weird. Kigali, Rwanda—things start to get dangerous. Bujumbura, Burundi—I might as well be on another planet.

The airport in Buja is a strange place. There was one flight a day at that time; sometimes the rebels took potshots at it. About twenty souls disembarked with me, including three children. We entered a terminal that looked like it was built for Disneyland in 1964 and then abandoned.

Half of the passengers were locals and breezed through customs, but the rest of us still needed a visa to get into the country. This was nervous-making because the plane almost immediately lifted back off for Kigali. I wondered what happened to you if they didn't grant you a visa.

We were given instructions in French. I don't speak French, but I imitated the other people who seemed to know what they were doing. I filled out a form, put it and the requested fee in my passport and gave it to a man who carried it away with all the others. It's scary when people walk away with your passport.

We waited. There were no chairs. The table where we filled out the forms was sprinkled with rat poop—big rats, from the look of it. This place must be fun at night. I waited 45 minutes after they took my passport away. One by one, the other passengers were okayed to go through. I was the last, and starting to think there is going to be a real problem, when the man finally came back with mine. I wondered if I forgot a bribe or something. Perhaps it was my absolutely virgin passport.

The official eyed me up and down, in my khakis, flowered shirt and African explorer hat; actually, I looked like I should be working at Disneyland.

"*Bon jour, Madame, parlez vous Frances?*"

"No, I have only English."

"You are here to teach?" He said in perfect English.

"Yes." I pointed to my official invitation attached to the form in his hand.

"You have not traveled outside the U.S. before this?"

"No, this is my first international experience."

He smiled and shook his head. "Bon chance, Madame, bon chance."

He waved me through.

Despite the company of my friend and host—the only person within 5,000 miles who knew my name—over the next few days I bumped into significant powerlessness. In the United States I am a competent woman. I am educated, professional, and comfortable in most settings. I usually know what I want and how to get it. In Burundi, I was nearly helpless. The list of powers of which I was stripped upon setting foot in the country was comprehensive.

1. Language: I didn't speak the local language or the professional language, and furthermore, I couldn't trust the non-verbal cues because the culture is just that different.

2. Self-care: I couldn't procure food, safe water, or even relieve myself without assistance.

3. Mobility: I could not drive. I did not know how to get to my house, or even back to the airport. I did not know the names of any streets. I did not know how to get a taxi.

4. Currency: I had no local money. I did not know how to exchange money. Credit cards do not work in this country.

5. Connection: I had no access to phone or internet. I couldn't phone home.

6. Cultural understanding: I did not know how to behave properly. I was aware that cultural blunders could be fatal.

7. Sexuality: I couldn't even smile and flirt with a stranger—my last-ditch defense at home. I did not know where the line was, and so it was not safe to use my female wiles.

I was a baby—a baby in a very hostile environment. I sat with that, telling myself that this was a good spiritual exercise. I was totally dependent on God and one good man.

Then I panicked.

When I was done panicking, I realized that I had one power left: the power to attend, to pay attention. And when I paid attention, I started to notice things, and then I learned. I noticed that when someone's name was said they responded with "*Ego*." They also said "*Ego*" when offered something good. I decided that "*Ego*" means, "Yes."

Soon, someone called my name, and I said "*Ego*," just as relaxed as you please. Everyone smiled and laughed, but I knew I had it right. They laughed and clapped with pride like you do when a baby says a new word. I was accepted. I belonged, and this is the beginning of power. I thought I was doing fine.

Then, on my third day, Niyonzima appeared at my door and announced that we were going up-country. I should pack a weekend bag. We were going for the conclusion of one of the first trauma healing seminars. His wife was there and we needed to pick her up.

We headed out of Buja to the south and followed the lake for most of the day. We traveled in our organization's big Land

Cruiser, but we are Quakers, pacifists, and so we had no guards or guns. Every gendarme and soldier, and a disturbing number of citizens, were all carrying assault rifles.

I asked David why we were not seeing the blue hats of UN peacekeepers. He told me that the UN had pulled them out a few weeks ago after a pitched battle in the suburbs. Apparently, the embassies were also empty.

We traveled on bad roads through beautiful country for most of the day. We were nigh unto the border of Tanzania when we stopped before turning inland and up. A cold Coke was produced for me, but I declined the roadside BBQ Beast, marinating in sun and flies.

Our driver asked how I was doing. I said I was fine, though my discomfort grew with the miles. I stated bravely that at least we hadn't seen any rebels today. He said, "We have crossed their lines twice—those fellows right over there are rebels." The rebels were enjoying the BBQ.

The road up to Makamba was dizzying. I didn't want to admit to being a nauseous rider. Makamba town was pretty, treed and colonial. Our people were waiting for us. They were ready for the finishing ceremony. I discovered my new primary role—prestige-raising decoration at ceremonies. More Cokes appeared.

At about what I thought ought to be dinnertime, I was taken to the New King's Hotel. I was well aware that I was getting the best of everything there; I was working hard on being grateful. My host said that he would give me some time to rest while he worked. As I was shown to my room, he drove off in the Cruiser.

My room was a concrete monk's cell. Six foot by twelve. It came equipped with a twin bed with clean sheets on a very dirty mattress with no pillow. There was a bare bulb hanging in the middle of the room. The tiny high window had bars to make me feel safe. There was a plastic lawn chair and a hook on the wall. The door had a latch, which was good, since there were spaces in between the slats of the door that you could stick a finger through. The bathroom was down the hall. It was communal, unisex, and filthy.

I told myself to chill. I laid down and tried to read. The sun set at six, as it does every day there. The evening got surprisingly cool. A fog of mosquitoes coalesced. I wondered if I was going to be fed. I wondered if anyone I knew would return. The hotel staff was sparse and I had not a word in common with them.

At about 9pm, cool as you please, Niyonzima and staff breezed in with supper on the veranda. I was working hard to learn to like bananas stewed with spinach in a soup of lukewarm palm oil. After that, I was wished a good night.

Everything that happened after this can be completely explained by hunger, exhaustion, jet lag, culture shock and Larium in my system. Take it that way, if you like.

I fell asleep fairly easily, but was awakened in the deep watch by the sound of footsteps outside my room. Someone walked up the hall, rattled the door of my room, walked away, then came back and rattled the door of my room harder. Probably just another guest counting doors to the restroom incorrectly, but it was the last straw for me.

I spun into a black hole of fear. I thought about screaming, but managed to hold it in. I knew that I was not in actual imminent peril. I tried talking myself down, but my sympathetic nervous system had gone into overdrive and was not backing down. Nothing to fight, nowhere to run.

That is when the whispering and laughter started. Mean, bullying, condescending laughter. "We finally have you where we can play with you." "No one who loves you has the first notion where you are right now." "We are very strong here. This is our court."

I tried to pray—every prayer I had ever been taught. My prayers bounced off the ceiling. My words choked in my throat. I tried to find the present Christ—access denied. I called for angels—none to be found. I cried like a baby for my mother. They liked that—easy to mock. It seemed distinctly possible that I was about to forget how to breathe. I got mad and cursed them—tried to command them away. Applause and more laughter. The room was hot and sticky and red. I curled into a ball and cowered.

But then I found myself speaking to The Mother. Words that I am sure I had never said before in my Protestant, Holiness life. "Hail, Mary, full of grace, the Lord is with thee, blessed art thou among women and blessed be the fruit of thy womb, Jesus. Holy Mary, Mother of God, pray for me. Pray for me. Pray for me, please."

And she did. There was another presence in the room, cool and sweet and blue. And I could breathe. The voices stopped. And were gone. There was a smell of light, fresh, dew-splashed flowers in the room. I sat with her, in quiet peace, with every good mother, confident and unafraid. Sweeping away vermin with the non-drama of a household chore. Unshakable, unquestionable love. It was so nice that I almost hated to fall asleep, but her lullabies are irresistible.

I am completely okay with labeling that night as a culture shock-induced, little psychotic break. Except that psychotic breaks don't usually end that well, and they don't usually leave you stronger. When I got up in the morning, I had a new level of confidence. Those voices have never tried to speak to me again, but since that night, I have had a relationship with a certain woman, that I can tap into whenever it suits me. And she prays for me, when I ask her to.

In Bujumbura

In Bujumbura, Burundi, there are about a million people in an area very much the geographical size of the Salem/Keizer metropolitan area where I live, a town of 150,000. The downtown is just about the same size as Salem's, but with residential areas going north and south along a narrow Lake Tanganyika. The slums are on the north and south edges. The air is dense and diesel-y. I knew my way around pretty quickly, which was a miracle in itself. There is not a single traffic control device in the city and very few street signs. Traffic was shared with long horned cattle, goats, bicycles and goats tied to bicycles.

Our house was on the south end, about five kilometers from downtown. Too far to walk in the ferocious August heat. But I could walk one klick to the main road and take a taxi cab for 3,000 Burundian francs. There were also taxi bicycles, and taxi motorcycles, simply called motos.

Niyonzima requested with great sincerity that I stay off the motos. He knew my predilections and temperament. His words to me were, "They die like flies—please do not make me call your father with bad news." That was the right thing to say to gain my submission.

There is no helmet law for passengers, but drivers must use them. They get their helmets from the market of Goodwill doom—anything that cannot be sold at the bottom of the first world barrel. Often, they wear unpadded plastic American football helmets from the 1950's, with no chin strap. They believe deeply in personal magic here.

The moto boys do like to look like badass bikers, and know that a jacket is required, so they wear any long sleeved jacket they can find: often down or fake down hand-me-downs from Green Bay, Wisconsin, near as I can tell. The aroma is not good.

Burundians are pretty hard to upset. They could teach stoicism in Sparta. Their little girls could teach tough to Klingons. They are masters of understatement, so it is good to know what things mean:

Hakuna Matata = Kiswahili for there is no problem. In American: you are on your way to the DMV.

Kama Kawaide = Kirundi for the ways things always are; the normal troubles. The most exasperating day you ever had at the DMV.

Challenging = The task will require persistence and possibly assistance. It's as if the DMV took five days, not one.

Interesting = a level of obstruction mystifying to even the locals. The DMV is being run by angry two year olds.

Activity = trouble, threat to security, possibly involving hand grenades. The DMV is being run by angry two year olds with guns.

A Situation = war, threat to life and limb, mass refugees. The DMV comes with land mines.

The Crisis = Genocide, presidents assassinated, millions killed. No one ever made it out of the DMV.

Trying to direct a taxi driver when you share no language can be challenging. When neither of you can name a single street in the city by name, it gets interesting. The streets of Buja have names. There is occasionally a sign here or there, but no one navigates by street names. They navigate by landmarks, and if you don't know those either, you have to get creative.

I knew the names of the major areas of the city. Our house is in Kibenga. The church is in Kamenge. I have French words for left and right, and a Kiswahili word for "keep on going." I never could find out the Kirundi word for "Stop." Kirundi does not have a word for "please." Their entire language and culture works in the imperative—commands all the time. If you want to be counter-culturally polite to a taxi man, you may use the French "*Si'l vous plait?*" But he will look at you with a look that says "What does my pleasure have to do with any of this?" We got where we were going, most of the time.

I saw some activity in 2003—the war was still on. On a couple of occasions, I was in a situation. My favorite internet café suffered a grenade attack. Amazingly, there were no serious injuries. *Kama Kawaide.*

My first African motorcycle encounter was with a man named Louis. I kept seeing him about town. He was the personal owner of a Honda Shadow 600, white with purple trim. He is a brave man because purple is considered the color of death by Burundians. There are very few personal bikes in Buja, (all the motos are commercial enterprises), so the Shadow was unusual just for that.

One morning, when I left the school where I was teaching, I saw the bike outside an internet café. It was being guarded by a small boy with a stick. Many people pay the street kids to watch their vehicles. It's a racket, but it is the customary racket. You don't want to make the street kids mad. They are tough at levels I don't like to contemplate, and after dark they are predatory.

I looked for and found the bike owner in the café. He had some English, and over Fantas, we swapped abridged motorcycle tales. The Shadow had come down from Kenya. He was one of those men who import hand-me-downs, which had made him rich. He offered me a ride. He was deeply interested in being seen with a *muzungu* (white) lady on his tail—very high status indeed. I checked in with my common sense, which said that on the back, I could be taken anywhere. And my father did not need any bad news. I resisted the temptation and obeyed wisdom. But the next time, I rode across town in Niyonzima's Land Cruiser, we crossed paths with Louis. We waved and shouted greetings. David looked at me, mildly concerned, and said, "Naturally you are friends—you are people of the same path."

My stay in Bujumbura included a lot of good work, even more fun, and a situation or two. David and I were briefly held at gunpoint by rebels, till he talked his way out of it—that was an exciting day. My alternative teaching gig at the Great Lakes School of Theology ended up including a student revolution. I was briefly the mother of a small nation of student families with 140 mouths to feed. I joined the rebels in that case. But we resolved that one with words as well. All the great revolutions start and end with well-spoken words.

Gitega

Be a sinner, and let your sins be strong (sin boldly), but let your trust in Christ be stronger, and rejoice in Christ who is the victor over sin, death, and the world.

-Martin Luther

Eventually, the war simmered down enough for me to get out of Bujumbura. It became safe to travel to some outlying areas. So I was upcountry, doing a three-day training. Upcountry is actually UP—the capitol is lakeside at the bottom of the Great Rift. The second city, Gitega, is in a high mountainous region. The road between them is fabled for bus plunges.

I was there to make beginning-level field traumatologists. I eventually made 40 of them, and David multiplied these like loaves and fishes into 400. They needed 4,000, or maybe 40,000, or 4 million—half the population—then everyone could help heal their neighbor.

One beautiful morning, we were in town buying breakfast. David's wife, Felicite', had gone inside a restaurant to buy *sambusa* (fried meat pockets—don't ask what kind of meat—we don't want to know) and Gitega doughnuts—cube-shaped fried bread. Upcountry, deep fried is the way to go for me—pretty safe. We were on the main square of town.

I was waiting at the truck with Emory, our driver, and my *charge d'affairs*, Daniella (David and Felicite's daughter), both teens. I got out and was conversing with a group of young Gitega moto taxi drivers. The country was becoming infested with cheap Chinese motorcycles. I had been practicing talking to the young drivers who stood in herds at intersections hoping for riders. We spoke a bad mix of Kirundi, English, French and Kiswahili, plus universal biker. The last worked best. I figured out how to tell them that I am in the club, and I praised their steeds and asked a lot of questions.

The bikes were all kick-start 125's. Noisy little hornets. The brakes and clutch are in the normal place but the shifter is a rocker instead of the straight up and down configuration of my Kaw. We were having a nice chat when I met the bravest young man in Burundi. He had a brand-spanking-new red bike. Chromed out. A treasure here; his livelihood, his manhood. He almost certainly didn't own it. He probably answered to a richer man who took a big cut of the fares.

And he looked at me and said, "*Muzungu*—You go?" He kicked the starter into life and pushed the handlebars towards me.

Oh, sweet Jesus, Mercy, a chance. Front seat, not back. After finding out that I had a friend in Buja with a bike, my host had again politely and sincerely asked/instructed me not to ride in Buja, as it was flat-out suicidal. But this was Gitega town square. Think post-apocalypse Mayberry.

The temptation was a black hole. I attempted retreat.

I smiled and said, "*Oya*, (No) not today,"

I turned away. I clutched my gut. I whined pathetically. Emory started shaking his head.

Dani said, "Resist! Peggy, Resist!"

I tried. I failed.

I turned. I walked over and sat on the running bike. We were on dirt with a steep little cliff up onto the broken edge of the tarmac. I was not too sure about the shifter. Dani got out of the truck, and stood in front of me.

"Peggy, no. Don't do this."

Traveling with an elder is an old Quaker tradition. While we recognize that no one can hear God for you, we also know that it is smart to listen to God with people as a balance. A truly immediate relationship with God always runs the risk of sliding into personal want and whim justified in the name of God. We try not to do this, really.

We like to pick our own elders for compatibility, but at need, a Quaker elder can also be anyone near you who is holding on to God better than you are in any moment. An elder is a governor on our unmediated spiritual engine. A grounded, sensible, 15 year-old girl, who happens to love you and who will tell you the truth makes a pretty fine elder.

My moral dilemma was clear to Dani, and she was eldering me in a very sensible way. Ignoring your chosen elder is usually a bad idea.

I knew this, and still it was not working.

I tried rubbing my nose in the stink of it to see if I could shame my way to sanity. If I crashed this boy's livelihood—even scratched it, I would really be doing a genuinely evil thing. I would be indulging my whim, my fancy. He could lose his precious, rare job; at the very least, he would be beaten. He probably supported others on the income—food to children.

I tried logic. If I crashed his bike, they would make me buy a new one at three times the going rate. I didn't have it, but I knew I could get it.

I tried fear. If I crashed me, the nearest hospital worth checking into was in Nairobi, Kenya, a thousand miles away.

Nothing was working.

I checked in with Jesus—He seemed to be laughing. I looked around for angels. They all had bikes. No one offered me a helmet, and the Gitega cops were all around, arms crossed, blank faces. It is against the law to not use a helmet. What could the fee/bribe be? 10 bucks tops—so worth it.

I said to Dani, "Baby doll, step out of my way. I am going to do this thing!"

She stepped aside, and started praying. In my khakis and African explorer hat, I nursed the bike up onto the pavement, such as it was, and took off. The hat blew off my head—fortunately, I have a stampede strap. My hair was blowing in the wind. Cars got out of my way. People screamed and shouted. It isn't every day, or every year, or every decade, that the locals get to see a white woman riding a moto in Gitega. Seriously, think bear on bicycle—Ringling Brothers comes to town.

I took her around the square at full tilt. I could not help the rebel yell that escaped my throat. I stood on the foot posts and whooped and hollered like a drunken cowboy come to town. Shops emptied of people.

It was then that I discovered that the front brakes didn't really exist. With great pressure, the rear brakes grabbed. I stood on them. I slowed back to where I started. I stopped in front of the Brave One. He was beaming. He was now famous. The taxi guys were shouting. The cops were applauding. I gave the bike back to the man with a nice Kirundi thank-you and a French, two-cheek hug.

I got back in the truck. Emory looked at me like I had grown an extra head. Dani praised God for His mercy. Then Felicity came out of the *sambusa* place and got into the truck, somehow without any clue as to what just transpired.

"Sorry it took so long," she said.

"*Hakuna matata*, Madame—please pass the *sambusa*."

No problem.

Inclusion

I like fresh road. Africa was the biggest and freshest road I had ridden at that point in my life. I came home with fresh eyes–fresh road does that. I came back with a passion for healing and for finding ways of escape through the barriers, obstacle courses, and mine fields that we use to keep people apart.

The love of fresh roads means that you stop where you can and accept help from whence it comes. People may be strange to you, but you can't let that make them into strangers. On the road at home, this often means other bikers.

The rift between the riders of Harley Davidsons and Japanese bikes is not as great as it once was. It used to be that if you pulled up to a watering hole in the middle of nowhere and a dozen Harleys were parked outside, you would ride your rice burner on down the road dry. It is still true that no self-respecting member of a patch-wearing motorcycle "Club" will ride anything non-American. But the biker code is real, and a biker of any stripe will stop and help another in need. However, you best carry your own tools.

Back east and down south you will still see cops on Harley Electra-Glides. But municipalities now feel free to get a good deal on Hondas without political repercussions. The State Police here in Oregon bought a stable full of German-made BMW's. Turns out they had to pick them up in Phoenix and ride them back home–so sad!

In the motorcycle world, like the rest of the world, inclusion and tolerance is becoming more normal. I believe that it will flourish naturally when we learn not to let someone rile us up for their own agenda —when we meet people as individuals, not icons. We can also plant seeds of inclusivity that germinate much later. As I age, I find these ancient sprouts popping up on a regular basis.

Throughout the turbulent 60's, in the turbulent city of my birth, I never heard my parents talk about ethnic groups in ways that painted swaths of people with the same brush. My parents talked about their co-workers as people, by name. I was often surprised to find out their ethnicity.

Sometime in my 20's, as my eyes were opening up to a fuller nature of diversity, I looked back on my childhood and saw six or eight gay teachers on my transcript; some were my mother's favorites. By then, it was the political 80's and the religious right was on the warpath about the homosexual agenda. They were great rilers. My mother was never much for the riling, so I worked up my nerve to open a conversation with her about it.

"Mom, did you know that Miss Cartier and Miss Hill were gay?"

"Well, I guess I presumed so, they lived their whole lives together."

"Did that seem unusual to you?"

"No, every community has had these people. Downstate we called it a Boston marriage, or funny uncles. They were often spinster school teachers or bachelor farmers. Once in a while, those spinsters would go off together to the mission field."

"It didn't bother you that a lesbian was my first and second grade teacher?"

"She was teaching to read and write, what did sex have to do with that? She was a wonderful teacher and you loved her, and you seem to be able to read and write."

She went on to tell me about a co-worker of hers at the teaching hospital where she worked. His name was Richard, and he was raised Church of the Nazarene—Holiness, like us—and he was a gay man. He latched on to my mother because she was kind to him, and they started watching the lunch hour soaps together at the university's student union. He had just come out to his parents and they had disowned him completely.

My mother was appalled. She could not fathom rejecting your child for any reason, let alone for something he could not change. She declared to me that it was the most un-Christian thing she had ever heard of. She said it was no surprise that Richard and his partner would not step into a church. She said it was a shame upon all churches. She did what she could; she tried to be his friend.

Welcoming someone, treating them no differently because of their difference, helping them when they are in need, staying in relationship, is all very near to the heart of the Gospel. It is also very subversive.

My mother did not live long enough to have a more important and personal discussion. In my 50's, when discussions of sexuality were even more open, and I knew, for myself, many queer folk, I started to ask more questions of myself and of the world. It didn't make sense to me that you couldn't be gay and be a Christian. It didn't make sense to me that it might be impossible to love someone, regardless of what body they happened to live in. I did not know why you couldn't ride a Harley one day and a Kawasaki the next. Why did we have all this choosing up of teams?

I had a long talk one night with a very open and thoughtful gay, Quaker friend. I described how it all seemed to me. He said, "Peggy, we have a word for that—it's called bisexual." It fit. It felt true. It also didn't change a thing in my life or relationships. It just made sense. And I started to be real interested in making sure that everyone got the chance to figure who they are, and to live that out honestly and authentically.

We live in the midst of a revolution of authenticity, and it is a good one.

When a Schism is not a Schism

**Who are these people
who are turning the world upside down?!?**

-Acts of the Apostles

I do love me a good revolution when I can get one. I hope sometimes that my headstone will read, "Mother of a nation—Hero of a revolution." Of course, it may just end up saying, "Says Who?"

One of the problems with human-made and human-led revolutions is that a remnant of the losers are always left smoldering, waiting for the chance to get revenge. A schism is when a revolution is ended by divorce. Large-scale schisms can often lead to fragmentation and the weakening of a people.

God-led revolutions are different. They aggregate rather than segregate. The victory is won through transformation, not through estrangement or subjugation. The worst kind of revolution is a human-led fight masquerading as a God thing. Attempted forced transformation. That sort of thing leads to an inquisition every time.

I came home from Africa ready for a revolution. But I wasn't dumb enough to try and manufacture one. Alivia and I had been talking about an unwavering craving to see something truly Quaker, and truly inclusive, and deeply Christ-centered. An oasis community where people could rest and recharge for whatever good work they did the rest of the time. Maybe even a church, not one that existed for its own sake, but one whose only purpose was to make some room for Mercy and Goodness.

Quakers, like every other piece of Christendom, have had their share of schisms. It happens a lot when you let humans in the door. It happens in every other area of human endeavor as well. We weren't really keen on starting another one, which was what would likely happen if we opened a church that had gay ministers and members. It would have riled our particular Quaker folks quite a bit.

Alivia and I belonged to a noisy, preachy branch of Quakerism that held onto the Jesus bit and the Bible bit pretty fiercely, but they were a little squeamish about inclusion. The other major part of Quakerism, where we had lots of Friends, was quieter and hanging tight to the no clergy thing, and the no dogma thing, but they were a little bit squeamish about the Jesus thing. We were clear that what we were being asked to pull together was going to challenge both parts of the Quaker continuum. I was called to be a pastor, I could not deny that. We were called to hold forth a creedless but real, historical, miraculous and present Jesus Christ. And the Revolution of Love, the full inclusion of God's queer kids, was right in the middle of it. Our dream had something to yank everybody's chain.

We weren't by any means the only Quakers or Christians thinking along these lines. In other places, people were ripping themselves apart at the seams over stuff like this. We oppose seam-ripping, whenever possible.

So we waited for the right time and place. We gestated. Every time I asked Jesus for permission to roll, He said, "Wait." I asked on a regular basis, like an apartment kid who wants a pony. Getting very similar results.

Then one Sunday, I found myself in San Francisco again. I was coming home from another righteous, rockin, radically inclusive service at Glide. I was on a BART train, deep under the bay. My friends were talking. I wasn't listening. I slipped aside and asked

Jesus, "Why not now? Why not like that, only Quaker?" And He was sitting right next to me, and seemed to take a second to consider, as if calculating a sum in His head, then said "Okay, now's fine."

I called back to Oregon as soon as I could get to a phone. "Liv! I have something to tell you!" "No, she says, you need to listen to me; I have something really important I need to tell you." I tried to get first tell, she told me to shut up. I did. Seems she had been to one of the quiet no-clergy meetings and a still small voice told her that she wasn't going to be doing traveling ministry anymore, that she would be settled in one place. She thought she was telling me bad news. She thought Sister Love's Traveling Salvation Show was over. She doesn't like to hold bad news. My reaction surprised her.

"But that's great! Cause I know what you are going to be settling into, it's gonna be an inclusive Quaker church called Freedom Friends."

It was her turn to say, "Says who?"

"Jesus, on the BART."

"Oh, well then, okay."

"You coming home anytime soon?"

So we did it. And because the time was right, neither side ended up mad at us. No fights were fought, no inquisitions held. We ended up being everybody's odd cousins. And we started aggregating a fabulous bunch of misfits, who needed a place just like that. Some have stayed, some have passed through, and some have gone back into other parts of the Quaker continuum to spread a lovely little virus.

Left Behind

My father left the planet to pursue other interests at the age of 88 years and a month. He stayed 16 years without my mother, and 12 years in my house. Guess that was about all he could take. I think he was a little nervous about seeing Mom again. He figured she knew the whole truth and nothing but the truth at this point. He wondered how that would play. We assured him that she had read him right from the get go, and accepted the whole deal.

On the day before he passed, I rummaged through a box of old stuff and found the plaque he had given me years before about roots and wings. I took it to his room and sat on his bed and said, "Thanks Dad, the wings were great. I'm gonna give them back now, okay?" He made ready to use them.

His passing was peaceful, and it didn't ruin me. I was close up and not far away like I had been for Mom. He was asleep, and so was I, when he went. The night nurse sent the night owl daughter up to wake me. I was just down into deep sleep and came up groggy.

"Mom—Grandpa's dead."

My reply was, "Says who?"

I prepared his body for the undertaker, and I was there the next day when they cremated what he had left behind. It seemed right to go with him as far as I could. We traveled home and hired an off-duty Chicago Police bagpiper, then put what was left of him into my mother's grave. We sang "It Is Well with My Soul" and read from the Apostle: "We do not grieve as those who do not have hope of the resurrection."

He left me some change. I started planning a return to Africa.

Dark

I do not often ride after dark. It is colder and I don't like to be cold. Visibility is poor—I won't see danger, and danger probably won't see me. More of the cagers are drunk. On long rides, ten hours in a day is about my limit and that usually comes before sunset. All good sense says, "Be in the barn by dark."

But sometimes sense goes AWOL. My dad taught me that sometimes you have to go out into the dark and the cold to see the really beautiful things. The dark also hides some spooky things. There is nothing like flipping up the face shield and howling at the full moon while flying. Some of the old cemeteries around here don't lock the gates at night, and sometimes you just need to talk to the old folks.

On the night that I found out that I was getting a divorce, against my wishes, and just shy of thirty years in, I went on a night ride. I howled. I cried—which is not good for visibility. I flew. I was a fury, mad at him and mad at myself. There was plenty of blame to go around. I was railing against the idea of being party to an action that would certainly hurt our daughters.

And then that quiet, not-me Voice said, "You'd rather give them a funeral to attend?"

I looked down at the tachometer and realized that I was red-lining it on a curvy, two lane back road, in country dark. Rosie's red-line is well over a hundred.

I hadn't been paying attention to road signs, but when the next crossroads pointed me to Scotts Mills, I took the turn, up past the town and church to the cemetery. I sat on the cold damp earth and had a talk with those little girls I still sometimes work for, the ones who hadn't managed to live through their parent's divorce, whose mother had died trying to get freedom for herself and for them. I called up my own parents—I felt the need to apologize. I also felt the peripheral presence of angelic friends.

And I listened to the Present Christ, who seemed quite sure that He wasn't done with me. Indeed, He quoted Himself, in the King James of my youth, and told me, "Woman, thou art loosed!"

I stood up straight and turned around, and went back, and took up my life. And eventually I found that the pleasant, fenced garden of my old life had a gate at the back, and when I walked through that gate I found a whole wild countryside of possibilities waiting for me.

Healing

"I am the Road, the Reality and the Revival."

-Jesus

Healing wants to happen. Whether physical, emotional, or spiritual, it is hard-wired into the motherboard of the universe. Spiritual healing is a natural consequence of time spent in the Presence of God. It will happen, unless we block it. The legion of ways that we block healing would be an interesting study, but it is not the topic at hand. When we attend to, care for, and nurture our soul we clear the pathways to healing.

It is critically important to remember that healing is a pathway, not an event. When Jesus said that He was the Way, the Truth and the Life, He was describing that pathway. Love is not a destination; it is a way of life. God is Love, an absolute equality in two directions. Where Love is, God is. What Love does, God does. So Love is the road, the only way to get anywhere meaningful. Love is tremendously realistic, true, authentic. It is also messy. You cannot love something without knowing its reality. Love always accepts what is. Then after acceptance, the life–the revival and healing start. There is no healing without love.

I was present when Alivia asked her cardiologist for the paperwork that would let her park in handicapped spaces. She had done a great deal of healing since I had brought her up to the Master back there in Santa Fe. She had accepted the reality of her whole self, including her sexuality. It is impossible to love

God and hate a part of yourself. She had decided to be a minister regardless of what anyone thought of that.

Alivia turned down the next round of chemo. Her lupus went into remission. She got her own motorcycle. We listened to the Voice when it told us that we could start a church for misfits and refugees. She went back to work. Liv still had a defective heart, but she decided to accept that, and do the things that she wanted to do anyway. She ended up being a pastor, and saves her energy for the things that are really important. So she made up her mind that it was okay to take the special parking space. The look on the doctor's face when she asked for a second sticker for her motorcycle was precious.

When I got around the accepting the reality that my good-enough-but-never-really-great marriage was over, I started to revive. That acceptance took a while—a lot longer than the divorce proceedings. Then I started listening to the voice of Love on the subject of my nearest relationships, and I realized that there was nothing that It could not do, no barrier that It could not transcend. So I relaxed and let a devoted friendship turn into a loving relationship.

Alivia and I were married at the Church on the Island of Misfit Toys (Freedom Friends Church, Salem, Oregon) in the spring of 2010. It was the best revival meeting I have ever attended. Alivia is now the pastor. I ended up being a pastor's wife.

Mother laughed.

Groups

The attentive reader will have already noticed this, but I like doing things by myself. I enjoy my own company. My inner world is at least as real as my external world. I am an introvert. This doesn't mean that I can't be a team player. And it does not mean that I cannot enjoy a group activity—now and then.

Like the rolling thunder group ride. Along with the cross-country solo quest, riding a bike with a group of other riders is one of the basic motorcycle experiences. You do not have to join a "motorcycle club" like the Hell's Angels, Disciples, or Gypsy Jokers to get this experience. If I had a regular crew, I would call them *Los Amigos Libertad*, which is the name of our church, because it sounds so boss in Spanish.

Like all group experiences, the group ride requires a special skill set. Managing distance and coordinating speed is critical. In traffic, you want a pretty tight formation; out in the boonies you want to string out to the maximum sight line for freedom and enjoyment.

Most groups who ride together regularly develop a set of hand signals. My favorite is "index finger straight up in the air, and then wag it in a circle" This means "rollers ahead" which only makes sense for "police presence ahead", if you remember the 1950's cop cars with the rotating bubble light on top. I've heard that some people who ride together get intercom systems for their helmets. Hands signals are way cooler.

Group riders also have roles. The rider in front sets the pace, watches for cops and other road hazards. Some people like to ride in the middle, which I think is the scariest place. One of the ways to get yourself seriously killed on a bike is riding in a tight formation and then someone stops suddenly or loses traction and goes down. You just about can't escape harm if you are in the middle of that scenario. Passengers often die first and worst.

By temperament and vocation, I like to ride sweep. That is the end of the parade. Mercy and Goodness' spot. I guess I am a natural sheepdog. I like to make sure everyone else is okay. The sweep can also choose their own pace, and you watch everyone and no one watches you.

OK, so, sweep is the introvert position as well. I am good with that.

But I led the pack once. A big pack too, on a grand road. One summer, I got notice of a charity run called The Pony Express Run. Female riders mainly from the East Coast were circumnavigating the continental U.S., raising money for breast cancer. At each day's stop, they gained new local riders who raised money by the mile. You could ride with them for a day or a week or a month, if you liked. On any one leg, the highest fundraiser got to lead the pack. The pack was some places as small as a dozen, in more populous zones, many dozens.

It was breast cancer that took my mother and my grandmother. The irony of using the bike to honor those two was too delicious to pass up.

I met the group at the California border and rode three days home with them. Fabulous gals (and a few guys). The core group was dedicating their whole summer to this thing. I got the honor of leading a pack of 24 bikes up from Roseburg to Crater Lake National Park and then back down to Eugene. There were Harleys and Ducatis and Hondas and Kaws, Beemers too. Very Inclusive—the people too, strong women and tender men.

The East Coasters were really impressed with the Cascade Range. Crater Lake has 10 foot snow drifts in mid-summer some years, and did that year. I had great fun pulling the leg of one Jersey girl. I told her that we had special snow out here that did not even start to melt till it was 75 degrees. Her science brain was skeptical, but the massive piles of white, barely sweating at 80, were messing with her mind.

Two dozen bikes in tight formation do make a tremendous roar. When we went through towns, we got a police escort and did not stop at red lights. The whole thing was pretty intoxicating.

The Book says that it is not good for people to be alone. We were made for community. Community requires you to put a governor on the engine of your inclinations. You can't cut the corners as hard; you can't open the throttle out in the same way. That is the grace you give to community in order to be part of it. You have to slow down and be willing to look twice. You have to be able to challenge your preconceived notions. It may feel like being tamed, but community can be tight and thunderous for the right cause. It can also be all strung out over the countryside, just barely keeping each other in sight. But you were meant to be kept in sight, and to watch out for others.

The church we built has been an interesting group ride. People have come and gone, much like the fundraising ride. I am not much for CEO-style, pastoral leadership. Quaker pastors tend to ride sweep. The group itself sets the pace, the pastor watches and listens, to lend aid to anyone who falls or breaks down. A pastor should carry a tool kit.

The homeless man walked in on a cold and rainy spring morning. Without the pack and just a little bit cleaned up, he could have passed for a Portland hipster. He was young, thin, and good-looking with a dark beard. He was welcomed, of course. He preferred cocoa to tea or coffee and gratefully spread his wet gear over chairs to dry. When we expressed our gratitudes, as we do, he said he was grateful that our OPEN sign was lit, and that it was warm and dry. He also said that his friend next to him was grateful. There did not seem to be anyone sitting next to him.

"Well, my friend cannot speak, because he is a squirrel, and way too young, as he has not opened his eyes yet."

It was not the first time that someone at Freedom Friends has brought an invisible friend to church, and we said that they were both welcome and that we were grateful to have them with us. I reflected that it was rare, and rather nice, for a hallucination to be something as gentle as a baby squirrel.

During our time for prayer requests, the young man asked for prayer for protection from whatever dark forces had magically stolen his Nilla Wafers in the night. He loved Nilla Wafers with pudding and had been saving them in anticipation of that joy, even though he did not have any pudding. He was sad about the loss.

At the rise of meeting, our new friend went back for a second cup of cocoa. He asked me if I wanted to hold his squirrel while he went to the kitchen. He held out a scrap of blanket. I decided I could hold an invisible squirrel for a minute or two. Then the scrap wiggled. With about four inches of furless, baby squirrel. As my preconceived notions shattered on the carpet, I looked again and saw homeless St. Francis and the true least of these.

I am not presently the pastor of Freedom Friends, so I was not the one who went out after meeting to buy an eyedropper and milk, along with Nilla Wafers and pudding.

Of Bits and Governors

A governor is a mechanical device that sets a limit on an internal combustion engine. Enforces a speed limit. They mostly get put on engines like trucks when the owner is not the one driving, and the owner doesn't actually trust the driver all that much. They are kind of like the bit in a horse's mouth–a threat at the tender spot, trying to control the source of power.

Some horses won't take a bit;–they don't get ridden much. Some horses don't need a bit. Reins, a well-placed knee, and a shift of weight are all they need to know what the rider wants, and they cooperate. No man has ever really owned a horse: they cooperate or not, the communication can be easy or mean, but if they work with you, it is because they want to work with you. It is a lucky horse that has a rider smart enough to know when the bit is not needed.

Butch Wheeler had a horse. She was a mare that he bought from the BLM. She was a descendant of a horse abandoned by a conquistador, or maybe one of the native people, liberated and lost. She was foaled into a herd, running loose out in eastern Oregon. When the herd gets too big, the government rounds some up and sells the healthy ones off. Butch named her Shiloh, after the civil war battlefield, I presume. Maybe he should have thought that over a little, because she fought him from the first day he had her.

Butch was the husband of a woman I knew who started a conversation with Jesus in a Quaker church and helped us start Freedom Friends. Butch was old school in many ornery variations and did not hold much with church. Butch worked for himself because he was too much of a cuss to work for someone else. Church people had not been good to him. He was not a fan of being told what to do. But Butch liked me, because I occasionally laughed at his bad jokes, and I took his teasing for what it was, an attempt at affection, and I gave it right back to him. He respected that.

One day. Butch and I were talking about fear. I told him I thought he was afraid of church. He dodged that by saying that I was afraid of his horse.

"Why would I be afraid of your horse?"

"Well, she's thrown me ten times so far, and she threw the trainer that I paid to break her, and this week she kicked the horse-shoeing man in the head. She'd throw you off her back in a second."

"I'm not afraid of your horse; in fact I'll make you a deal. If you come to church and hear me preach, I'll come that very day and ride your horse!"

Butch laughed. "That'll never happen."

And so it seemed. Months went by, and then one day, out at Scotts Mills, that old man walked in late, took his hat off, sat on the back bench and grinned the devil's own grin at me while I preached. I was a wee bit intimidated.

After meeting, I greeted Butch and said, "I'll just go home and get my boots and jeans and I'll meet you at your place."

He laughed and said, "Sure is gonna be fun to see you land on your head; try and miss the rocks, okay?"

An hour later, I was at the man's ranch. I am a fair horsewoman, but not good enough to ride a wild horse. I figured I was going to get bucked off, but it seemed a good thing to do for the sake of the Gospel.

"I'm here. Saddle her up. I'm gonna take a ride, even if it is a short one"

Butch laughed long and hard, enjoying his joke and my bravado–and then he said, "I didn't really mean it–you don't have to ride her."

"No way—a deal is a deal."

"Seriously—we'll saddle up a couple of the others and go for a ride, okay?"

"Not a chance. You get her out here."

So he brought out the wild mare, and put a saddle on her. She only tried to kick him twice. Butch's wife was looking daggers at him.

"Really, Peg, you don't..."

I took the horse by the halter and let her breathe my breath, and I said to her.

"Shiloh, is it? This old man, who does not own you, does not know that the word means, 'that which belongs to God.' So it is for you. Free you were born, and free you are, but I happen to work for your true owner, and I would appreciate it if you did not throw me off today."

I got up on her and we walked out into the pasture, and I made sure that I used a gentle knee and neck reined without putting any pressure on that bit.

Butch yelled, "Hold those reins tighter!" I did not.

And she took me once around the pasture, and she trotted and cantered like a lady. Then, like a person with a brain, I got off of her.

Butch's jaw was slack and his eyes wide.

"I'll be damned," he said. "I think probably not," said I.

Me and Butch and Shiloh, and probably Rocinante, are all of a breed. We don't care for the bit and avoid those who would slap an external governor on our engine.

There are a lot of religions that are all about the external control. Quakerism is more trusting. With enough unmediated time with the Creator, the control becomes internal. That is the bet we make. God will not use a bit. We cooperate and get ridden or we languish in the pasture, thinking we are free, but really just being idle.

I do not want to be idle.

Sin

She just wanted to talk. Over coffee or something after we finished the shift.

People used to ask me to do that a lot when I was in my twenties. I was a young mother waiting tables to put the baby's father through school. I worked swing. We passed the baby off at the door most days. The baby thought it was great to trade in for a new playmate when the other one got tired.

I was often late coming home because my co-workers, and sometimes customers, wanted to talk to me. They had troubles, and apparently I could listen and sometimes say something useful. Or ask a good question. Or just tell them that it was going to be okay. I liked what I was starting to think of as my second job. It felt right to me. It made me feel pretty good to do it. Feed the bodies, feed the souls.

One night my husband said, "You know, people do this for a living. I think they get paid more than waitresses." He was right, and their feet don't hurt so bad.

Crystal wanted to talk. I didn't really care much for Crystal. She was lower class, sometimes crude. She probably bought her hair dye at Dollar Tree. We didn't see eye to eye on politics or religion or much of anything. I knew my waitress days were numbered, but I was pretty sure she would be doing this when she was old.

And she wanted to talk. She asked in front of one of the other girls. It was a thing I was known to do. Everyone knew Crystal had troubles.

I suggested Denny's. She wanted to go to that new place that had the fancy coffee. We got our coffees from the chichi coffeemaker who refused to call things what they were. I couldn't figure out what was suddenly wrong with small, medium and large.

We sat. I drank my coffee-in-milk that was so fundamentally different from milk-in-coffee. I waited for her to open up. I was patient. She didn't touch her three-dollar coffee. She finally looked at me and took a risk. "I don't really like coffee," she said. "It just buffs my scene to be seen here." She spent a lot of time looking around to see who was seeing her.

She wanted to talk about being a mom. She had five kids already. She was trying to earn enough to make it six. Because six was her lucky number, and a mother of a half-dozen was a big freakin' deal. But she was worried, because her boyfriend—dad to some—had taken up the crack again. And he was mean. And he let creeps come over while she was at work. Except for sometimes when he just forgot about the kids and left. This bugged her, because she really worked hard to be a good mother, ya know? And he was really kind of embarrassing; she couldn't take him anywhere nice. But she had always had a soft spot for him, and she thought he was sexy. She wondered what she ought to do about him.

But she didn't ask me about him. She asked, "You think I'm a good mom, right?"

"Who's watching the kids right now?"

"He is... probably."

So I let her have the truth. I let her have it. I told her that I thought she was a terrible mother. That I was thinking about going home and calling Children's Services in the morning. I told her that the last thing she should be thinking about was breeding another kid with that loser.

She gave me back the exact string of profanities that you would have expected, and walked out. We never spoke again.

I went home to my Christian household, a bit riled up, but righteous. I had spoken the simple truth in defense of defenseless children. I would later uphold it as prophetic ministry. Sometimes love is tough. Somebody has to be willing to point out the ugliness others ignore. Right?

It is possibly the biggest sin I have ever committed.

Because I knew what I thought she deserved, and I also knew what she needed. She needed to be valued. She needed to belong. She wanted to love and be loved. I knew that she needed to find a way through, a way of escape. She spent most of her time and thought trying to create a beautiful, fragile, bubble of pretty. She had a world full of people to tell her she was ugly, and stupid—people happy to pop her bubble. And she thought that maybe I could help her make her bubble better.

And I hit her bubble with a sledgehammer. Because I could. Because it buffed my scene to be that much better than her. Because some part of me liked the power that she was handing over to me, and I intended to wield that power.

The sin I committed is called contempt, and it is the mother of every sin. In it, I hold you to be of less worth, worthless—certainly beneath me. You are someone who can be hurt, or quietly mocked, or ignored completely, with impunity.

Each and every one of the Big Ten sins starts with contempt. It is a form of blasphemy, because God says, "It is good" and I contradict God and say, "Not so much." You cannot start a war without contempt. You cannot crush a heart without it. We gild our contempt with religion, and intelligence, and a hundred other sugar-over-shit glazes.

And the worst of it is not the injury inflicted. It is the grace withheld. For each and every time that I am aware of the choice to speak grace or contempt, and I choose contempt, this universe is impoverished and set off the track of glory. Grace extended becomes matter, it becomes real and imperishable. Grace withheld can never be retrieved. We can only make a better choice the next chance we get. The cumulative effect of a bazillion graces withheld is the only thing wrong with this world. And it is very wrong.

It is rape when the other choice is protection, revenge when the other choice is forgiveness. It is offering a polite excuse or feigned busyness when the other choice is attention. It is taking the moral or political high ground when the other choice is relationship.

I don't think that God cared a bit about my childhood apostasy. I actually think that God was on my side in that one because the god that I was railing against was a false god of punishment and fear and hypocrisy. The Real Deal is against that stuff too.

I also think that my God is pretty understanding when I cave in to temptations. There is a part of every temptation that is a backwards nod to something that was created to be delightful. God gets that.

God is real close to me when I engage in rebellion and debauchery, working hard to find me a way of escape. God is not in a matter/ anti-matter relationship with sin. Nothing blows up. God does not do a cosmic face palm of disappointment. God gets into it with us, and gets us through it, and out of it, if we cooperate even a little.

But there is not much that God can do with a grace intentionally withheld.

A lot of people in my childhood tried to scare me with a boogeyman they called the anti-Christ. None of them was ever mean enough to tell me that I carried the anti-Christ in my mouth. Even the hellfire preachers had a little more grace than that.

Love—Insistent, Persistent and Militant

"Mom," said little Peggy, "How could you be happy in Heaven if someone you loved was in Hell?"

"That's why we work and pray so that everyone we love can be saved, Peggy."

"Yes, but Mom, not everyone accepts Jesus. What if someone you love, really love, doesn't get saved?"

"That is the saddest thing that can happen, Peggy"

"But I thought there was no sadness in heaven; the Bible says all tears will be wiped away."

"Heaven will be happy."

"Will you remember me in Heaven, Mom?"

"Of course I will, honey. You will be right there with me!"

"What if I wasn't saved?"

"You've accepted Jesus, Peggy. Are you worried about that?"

"Not really, but what if I did it? What if I rejected him? Would I go to Heaven? Could you be happy in Heaven if I was not there?"

"The Lord would have a way of working that out."

"How, how would He make that OK?"

"I don't know. Peggy... I guess a person's memory would be cleansed of their loss."

"You mean you would forget all about me? How can you call it happy, if a mother has to forget her own children?"

"I could never forget you, Peggy."

"I know, Mom, that's why I am confused."

She changed the subject and gave me a hug and a kiss and sent me off to bed. Then I am sure she talked with my dad, and that they prayed for their children.

I didn't like the memory-wipe theory of eternal happiness then, and I don't like it now.

I don't believe in separation any more. I just don't believe in it. If God is Love, then all Love is of God. Where Love is—there God is—without exception. If you truly love, or are loved, by anyone, then God is in that relationship, named or unnamed. God touches them through your love. And because God is love, and God is indestructible, as long as you love them you cannot lose them. Separation by distance or even death is an illusion at best, and at worst a destructive lie.

I am persuaded beyond doubt that neither death nor life, nor angels nor any other powers, nor height nor depth, nor anything else in all creation can separate us from the love of God. (Romans 8)

The only way to end up in Hell is to neither love nor be loved. That is a rare but terrible fate in this life. It takes work to disconnect so completely from others. And even then, some one of them may love you still, so the thread of love is still there. But even if you managed to achieve that level of disconnect from every other human, and all humanity had rejected you—Well, then, there is God. And God loves you, and knows where you are, and you are not and never will be, lost.

God will not force you to be close. But even if you isolate yourself in some furthest reach of darkness, that one cord of love is still there, and you have the option of taking hold of it and using it as your road map home. You can reel yourself in. I see absolutely no reason to believe that this option ceases to be available due to an arbitrary marker such as death. I am, right now, connected by a cord of love to more people in Heaven than I can count. My connections to Heaven get more numerous every year. At the same time, I am braiding cords of love with as many people here as I can. I am regularly overcome with love for some of my students, and clients, and people I only hear about. I remember them.

If Love works like this, then our job becomes not to convince as many people as possible of our version of the Truth, but to love as many of them as we can, as well as we can—especially the ones who are hard to love. We need to love across every boundary, every border. Love across doctrine. We need to love across party lines, and love across economic class. We need to remember people, in our hearts and thoughts and prayers. We practice our litanies of love. So that when we take our place in the eternity of God's love, without these brains and bodies, those fiber optic cables of love will stretch across oceans of time and space and pull in as many as we can.

I want to love like the Marines fight—No bodies left behind.

Part 5:
Way Opens Wide

No, my adventures are not "safe"—that is the point. This world is not safe and an unmediated relationship with it and its creator will never be safe. I accept this. I also refuse to let it limit me. I refuse to worship the idol of safety. She is a bitchy and demanding goddess. She drinks blood. She is the kind of goddess that can only make herself big by making you small and smaller. She loves padding. She loves mediation between you and everything Real and Divine. She muffles, sedates and cushions Heaven and Hell both. She wants you asleep at the wheel. My tribute to her is small and begrudged. But never think that ignoring her will not piss her off. It will, and she will try to sink your boat.

Madame Moto-Muzungu

In 2010, two months married to an indulgent spouse, Africa rang up again, and asked me to come, this time to do some work with the young people at Kamange Friends Church. The government had gotten mad at the French again, and there was an English-based East African community forming up around Anglophone Kenya and Tanzania, so Burundi decided that all its university students should have English. Immediately. After teaching them for twelve years in French.

There were some young people who I cared about, stuck between a Rift and a hard place. I didn't have enough francs or shillings for the trip, so I made a hard choice. I sold Bucephalus. Pert near truth be told, it was too big for me, and too fast. I had control, but never mastery. I was going to die, not on that bike, but somewhere in its vicinity. So I very sensibly turned it into cash and took a nice, safe, 1000-mile solo trip on the people's busses from Mombasa, on the Indian Ocean, through Kenya, Uganda and Rwanda, back down to Burundi.

It's really hard for me to do any business in Burundi. I have a hard time buying bananas. I have a toddler's vocabulary in Kirundi, and less in French. I can count the fingers on one hand in either language, but I often get stuck on four. Money comes in denominations of hundreds and thousands and millions. Even street sellers negotiate in French. The price of anything negotiable—which is almost everything—triples or more when I look at it because I am *muzungu*. Since I do not know how much things ought to cost, all I can do is roll my eyes, cut the price in half, wave my hands, shout a bit, and hope. At the end of the day,

I check my purchases with the children. They laugh and beg me to send them, and to not try and buy things myself. Daniella is a great bargainer and for anything important, or expensive, I send her. There is not really anything that requires much more skill than that. All my basic needs are supplied by my generous hosts.

But once in a while, I just get notional.

It was my first Sunday morning in Burundi. I was feeling confident and settled. We were on our way to Kamenge Friends Church. Mother Feli was driving. Niyonzima was in Nairobi for the week. He was on airplanes, being a sensible human. I was re-orienting to daily life in Bujumbura. I was quizzing Feli on the cost of the basics, as inflation was dizzying. A taxi to downtown? Don't pay more than 3500 francs.

In 2010, the population of motos in Buja had risen exponentially. "What do the motorcycle taxis cost?" "Oh, Peggy, please don't ride the motos—they really are not safe." And then the voice of Dani's brother Yoyo, from the back seat—"Unless, of course, you are driving!" Everyone in the car laughed, because it was ridiculous.

A gong sounded in my belly. That evening, I sat on the terrace, watching the sunset over Lake Tanganyika, made all the more spectacular by the terrible summer air pollution. And I had a little chat with Jesus about motorcycles. The conversation ended with me telling Him that if He did not want me on a bike in Buja, that I would submit to that, but that I was going to make a few inquiries and see if way opened.

"Way Opening" is a concept that Quakers are particularly fond of. It is a deep trust of God and God's universe. If you are supposed to do something, it will become possible to do it. You may push a little, but if Way does not open, you also accept that.

The first problem with my plan was that I could not make inquiries among any of my friends and acquaintances because, except for Yoyo, there seemed a clear sense that Peggy should stay in taxis. And Yoyo would probably flip on me if he found out I was serious.

The next problem was money. I knew I could not afford to buy a moto, even the little Chinese bikes that were the entire market there, and I was pretty sure that I did not have budget for a lease or rental. I had a Visa card, but it had failed at an ATM in Kenya—at a tourist resort. Businesses don't take them at all in Burundi, but you can go to the big bank and withdraw a cash advance, if they recognize your card.

I decided to walk into a bank and see about a transfer. A nice young man said it was possible, but he had to go several steps up the chain of command to find someone who knew how. My card was inspected by four different bank managers. They had that ka-chunk-style machine to make a mimeograph of my card. They called my number in to the main branch—and they received approval to try and get me 500 USD. The good news was it would only take three days for the transaction to occur. They seemed very excited about their success.

The next problem was time. I had already spent half my time in Africa. I had about six weeks left. Making a major purchase and getting a vehicle licensed and insured could easily take up all that time. I did not expect to succeed, so I felt at liberty to try.

So the next morning, I walked up to the main road, and besides getting a moto ride downtown, I managed to find out what the moto boys (yes, they are mostly boys—teenagers) pay per day to rent their bikes. They are vehicular sharecroppers. Someone else owns the bike; they have a daily fee to pay and get to keep anything over. The market was so flooded that if they gave six rides in a day, it was a good day.

We traded this knowledge by writing in the dirt, and a combo of Kiswahili, French, Kirundi, drama, charades, and one sharp moto boy who finally grokked that I did not want to rent a bike and boy for the day, I wanted to rent a BIKE for the day. When I asked if any of them would rent me their bike for a day at a small mark-up, they laughed me into the dust. But I did get a ride downtown and a piece of information. They pay 10,000 Burundian francs a day (about $8.50.)

Arriving downtown, I had a few other errands, and I intended to just walk into a few bike shops and make some inquiries. Motorcycle taxis are a huge industry in Buja and there are quite a few shops that cater to the trade. Relatively few motos are privately owned and ridden: why ride when you can clear 10k by letting it out?

I went one block and looked up the street. And there was "MIRACLE MOTORS–SUZUKI MOTORCYLES–AVE de la REVOLUTION." Jesus chortled.

I walked in and they had real Japanese bikes assembled in India. One million-eight to buy (just under two grand USD.) The proprietors looked bored, and the owner, one Mr. Muni Raju, greeted me in English. Indian businessmen are common in Buja. God bless the British Empire–long may she stay dead!

I told him my situation. I asked him if he thought it was conceivable that I might lease a bike for six weeks. He looked me up and down, smiled a small, indulgent, wicked grin, and said, "See this one, my friend just bought it to rent out as a moto, the six weeks needed for documentation should be finished in a day or two, perhaps I could call him and see if he would like to rent it to you?"

Mr. Muni Raju received the kiss on the cheek with great dignity. I told him I could pay 10 thousand Burundian Francs per day for 38 days. He told me to come back in the morning and he would let me know.

And I walked out and considered these things in my heart, with only the occasional smirk.

The next day, the moto boys near our home greeted me with mild derision.

"Still walking, *Madame*?"

I told them that they needed to have more faith, and bought a ride. I tried to get the boy to let me drive and give him a ride, double pay, but he scoffed. I do not think he believed that I knew how. Plus, the humiliation of being seen behind a woman would have probably killed him.

At Miracle Motors, the news was solid and good. Mr. Benjamin Mutua, a Kenyan and a teacher at Hope Africa University (where David teaches, and Feli and Dani study) had agreed to rent to an unknown American lady—but he asked to meet me.

He received the kisses on both cheeks with great dignity. When he found out that I was a Quaker pastor, he was stunned, and asked after David. I told him that he was out of the country. The university was on break and I just hoped that Mr. Mutua didn't have Feli's cell. He told me that the bike was all insured, documents paid for and that it should be ready the next day after a visit to the DMV for an inspection. He called his wife and told her the news of his novel sponsorship and took pictures of me, and us, and the bike. We agreed that if I wanted to take riders that the fee should be five times the normal—ten if they wanted to hang on tight! He promised me there would be a line. (We were kidding—I was not getting the commercial license.)

I walked to the bank and had $500 USD in my hands in no time—Better than half a million francs.

I slept under my mosquito net with a smile on my face, but told no one, for fear that a call would be made to Nairobi to get the only human voice in Africa with the power to command me.

The next day, the moto boys were kinder, as I had obviously failed. At Miracle Motors, the bike had a new shiny license plate and the mechanic drove her off to the DMV. While I waited, a bearded and burly *muzungu* gentleman parked a vintage British bike out front and walked into the dealership. He only boggled at me a bit. I boggled extensively back at him. He introduced himself as Kenny Johnson and claimed to be a native-born inhabitant of the country. Naturally he knew Niyonzima.

With great trepidation, I shared my plan with him. He opened his pack and took out a battery-powered blinking light and told me to take it as a gift, and to wear it on my person when riding. He seemed to have no concern for my safety beyond that. He told me to look him up if I had any need. No reason to give me an address, as everyone knew Mr. Kenny Johnson and anyone could point out the way. "It is so." Said Mr. Raju.

After four hours of waiting, the bike came back. As a final little funny, they had covered the commercial moto sign with a rainbow sticker. The angels giggled.

Mr. Mutua arrived for the christening. Mr. Raju finally got a little nervous and asked me if I needed driving lessons. I declined. I did practice the kick-start, but she leapt at the first chance to start for me.

As I rode back to the house, I made sure to stop and visit the moto-boys, who in great Burundian form immediately swallowed their skepticism and shouted an Africa HUZZAH! All hail the great Madame Moto-Muzungu of Bujumbura! I was their new patron saint. I was expecting small plastic statues of a white lady on moto to appear on moto dashes as soon as they could be ordered from China. Such was their reaction.

When I got to the house, I beeped several times, until Yoyo finally looked out the gate. The look on his face said it all: "Be careful what you speak, Yoyo—the Lord seems to want to make you into a prophet!"

Daniella rolled her eyes at me, but her first question was if they had given me two helmets. They had. Feli made an African mother protest, but she didn't really put her heart into it—I have seen the real thing. Our houseman asked for small change to acquire polish. When David got home from Kenya, he had clearly been warned. He was all cool confidence and unsurprise.

I thought about the motorcycle I had sold to get here. I cast my bread upon the water and in due time it came back to me divided by ten, if you count cubic centimeters; multiplied a thousand times if you are counting joy. I named her Milagro.

The WAY of Traffic

African traffic is a complex integrity. The Traffic, she is one, yet many. You must understand her and honor her as one, yet participate as one of many. You are part of her; this you must accept. If you attempt to enter her as a solitary being, she will reject you. You must become her, while being true to your own nature.

The various parts each have their own nature. The great lorries are the *tembo*, the elephants. They embody power. They start slowly and stop more slowly yet. They rumble where they will. They do not adjust or change their course for you. To ask them to make any sudden change or even to notice you is to ask them to be untrue to their own nature, and the Traffic, she will be offended. Nothing good ever comes of that.

The autos, great to small, are the cattle: bulls and cows. The big Land Cruisers push aside the smaller cows. It is their nature. Cattle move best in orderly formation, they queue up rank and file. Autos respect lorries and make orderly rows around them. They pay attention to the lorries and notice their intentions to turn or stop. They attend and cooperate. When they are true to their natures, they move with regularity and intention; neither timid nor impulsive. If a large auto thinks to take upon itself the nature of the lorry, Traffic will eventually teach that auto a lesson in humility. When the auto is fearful, and does not live up to its rightful place, Traffic will be confused and frustrated.

We are the moto. We swarm. Our nature is quick and intuitive. We are like water, and flow into the spaces left by the larger creatures. We are like smoke, and rise to the top of every queue.

The lorries do not see us. We are beneath their recognition—sometimes we are beneath their tires. We pay homage to them, not the other way around. The autos cede us our place and are not offended when we pass them and form up at the front.

It is in our nature to form groups whenever we can. A swarm of motos can move as one and be recognized as a cow to make a left turn, and then we melt again into a string and thread our way through. When we are untrue to our nature, and in a solitary act of hubris attempt to take the place of a cow, the cows are offended at the waste of space. If we are true to our nature and listen for the voice of Traffic, she will reveal a pathway for us and maintain our safety in it. It is untrue to our nature to attend to the lower creatures, but it is in our nature to announce our presence frequently with our bright chirping horns, so that the lower creatures may honor us.

The bicycles are a fallen race. Once they swarmed, dipped and dived like the moto. Now, they have been pushed to the edges. Working harder for so much less. Not able to compete in size or speed, they sell their sweat, and dream of the upgrade from caterpillar to butterfly. It is a kindness, an alms-giving to make way for the bicycles—a payment in humility to the knowledge that Traffic is not done creating and someday you may be moved to the edge.

The humans walk. They have their own pathways now on the concrete ways. It is wrong to drive on their path. When Traffic sings her song in the dirt, they join us in the way. It is important to sense their presence but not really see them. They are watching the moving ones. Gaging their nature, speed, and attitude, and finding their own path. If you look at them and try and adjust to them, it will just throw them off and plunge them into peril. They trust you to stay true to your nature and you must trust them to protect their own lives. They are occasionally skittish and they balk or jump. When this happens, you must look at them and try not to kill them, but Traffic is disturbed and their peril shifts to you as you deviate from the way. You must regain harmony as swiftly as possible and thank Traffic for the grace.

Traffic does not walk, or sweat, or swarm, or queue, or rumble. She flows. Serene when all who are part of her surrender, accept, and engage.

Glory or Death

I had a wardrobe problem. I had not brought along any shoes fit to be a motorcyclist. At home, I wear heavy leather boots to mid-calf. Even if I had my boots, they would have been too hot. I could not even think about a jacket, but with bare ankles next to a hot motor and on streets like a dirt-bike track, I was going to be hobbled in no time. I looked all over town. Nothing.

One day, I saw a boy in Chinese knock-off, fake Converse high tops– now that was the ticket. He told me where he got them and I found the shop of all things cool and fake. Every brand name you would ever not want, in cheaper form. And yes, they had the shoes of the basketball men—"Real NBA" fake Chucks. And they came in black and they said on the side in gothic lettering "Glory or Death." I was told that I would never get them back through US customs because they would be confiscated. I was told this by many fellows who wanted my shoes. I didn't think there was any chance they would last that long.

Subversion—African Edition

I believe that God has hidden God's self in every culture and people. But where God goes, evil follows. Evil is actually better at following God than we are. And evil has sticky roots. So every culture must be compared to Gospel Culture, Gospel Order, as Friends name it, and some parts are to be treasured and some parts eradicated. Mind you, I am not unaware of how badly my own culture needs this. And I speak to that as well, but my call is more apostolic than that. I care about the bigger picture. I care about how all the pieces fit together. When God shows me a piece that needs fitting, I work on it. Working with victims of torture, child soldiers and genocide survivors had made a few things clear about some pieces of the central African culture that could use some work.

Burundian culture is much closer to the Biblical culture of Jesus' day than is our own. They really know from sheep and goats, for instance. One of the cultural beliefs that they share with that place and day is the notion that if anything is going bad in your life, the first thing to consider is how badly God is mad at you. Natural disasters are God's wrath, what else?

My young students in Buja had great science knowledge for their age in some categories, Chemistry for instance. Earth science, not so much, so I built environmentalism into our curriculum. But my underlying agenda was their theology. They, like many of us, are not accustomed to finding theology under the microscope. Silly us.

When we got to greenhouse gasses, my students could give me the chemical notation for methane. When I asked them what caused earthquakes, the answer was God. This is a problem because they live on the Great Rift, and one-third of my class wanted to be architects or contractors. They knew the name of the Rift, of course, just not the implications of that rift. The bottom of that rift was a few dozen kilometers from us at the bottom of Lake Tanganyika. There had been a good-sized quake in Bukavu, DRC, 100 klicks north in the last decade, but none in Buja in these kids' short life spans. When I posited, as a near certainty, the occurrence of a quake in Buja in their lifetimes, most of them shook their heads, some laughed. A couple, including Dani, looked concerned, as I have a bit of a rep as a prophet in those parts. I made it clear.

"I do not have this from God, I have this from science."

"It cannot happen here," one said.

"Why?"

"Burundians pray too much—we worship so beautifully."

"Do not the Congolese in Bukavu pray?"

"The Congolese are wicked—this is well known—they rape their own women in Bukavu. God is angry."

"Ah, good, then there is no rape in Burundi. That is good."

It got very quiet.

They had heard the story of Hurricane Katrina, of course, and the God's wrath explanation of it. I told them more of the story. How every little church in the ninth ward was destroyed and how the wicked French Quarter stood high and dry. How the black people died and the white people escaped. "Racism!" they cried. "What? You do not think God was mad at the little churches and their black worshippers?" I told them that the rich escaped and the poor did not. "*Kama Kawaide*."

"So God is not mad at the poor?"

And I took them to the Gospel of John, where they ask Jesus who sinned, the blind man or his parents. And Jesus says, "It's not like that." I asked them what the Sermon on the Mount had to say about the contractors in Buja who mix too much sand in their concrete to save money. When the rains come, these buildings melt, so what will happen to them in an earthquake?

Will that be God or man?

We had a long moment of Quaker silence.

Providence, Burundi

The lesson I was teaching that day at the young adult leadership conference had been from the Sermon on the Mount. "Do not worry about what you will eat or what you will wear; your Father in Heaven knows what you need." I had listened to student testimonies of provision. One student spoke of being at boarding school with no pocket money when the whole school went on short rations of one meal a day with no meat or veggies due to a budget shortfall. That is what African boarding schools do—short of money? Stop feeding the students. Hungry, the student said that she walked into a nearby vacant lot and found that it was abundant in wild cucumbers. God is Good.

Teacher had a different need that day. Milagro the Moto had become increasingly difficult to start. It had taken 37 kicks to get her going the morning in question. I had taken her in to Miracle Motors for a check-up, and the young mechanic had declared her fit and Mr. Muni Raju had taken pains to re-educate me about the kick-start process. The starting problem was declared to be mine.

I disagreed. I had borrowed younger male legs, and I had borrowed experienced moto legs, and they had no better luck than I. Mr. Raju respectfully suggested that my femininity was a problem. I almost respectfully asked Mr. Raju to demonstrate starting the bike with his male bits, but thought better of it. I pointed out that the bike was idling very low. Mr. Raju agreed with this, but told me that I should just ride with the choke on all the time. I knew this was bad advice, and that I was fouling the plugs enough as it was, and she was still stalling at stops on a regular basis. And in Buja, every time she stalled, I had an immediate throng of amateur mechanics and riders offering me advice in Kirundi, often all but pushing my feminine self off the bike to show me how it was done. This was irritating. I needed a second opinion.

I assessed my limited resources, then remembered the man I had met on the day I had acquired Milagro. I had found out that Mr. Kenny Johnson is indeed the Burundian-born son of Plymouth Brethren Missionaries—Holiness people. He is also an owner and restorer of a stable of vintage bikes.

Three weeks after our meeting, I desperately wanted to have a motorcycle chat with someone knowledgeable and neutral. I especially wanted to have this chat with someone who did not consider it to be an abomination against God or the gods for me to sit my female self on such a machine. I decided to find him.

After class, I started asking about him, and *et voila,* in no time, I had a phone number for Mr. Johnson. He was home, and we were welcome to stop by. We were warmly received by Ken and his assistant, Deo. (In a Francophone Catholic country, lots of people have Latin names, Deo Gratias is a common one—Thanks be to God—which gets shortened to... God.)

Kenny and God had a truly fine and complete motorcycle repair shop. We took Milagro apart. The idle and the idle mix were both off. The plug was filthy from running so rich. Several bolts, including the one holding the shift rocker pedal, had been worked loose by the daily dirt-bike track that was our neighborhood. Finally they discovered that the shift cable was slipping. All these things were adjusted. Every bolt tightened. Tire pressure adjusted. Ken test-drove her. I started her with the crew watching. She started on kick number two—good enough.

I expressed my profound gratitude to God, Kenny, and God, and started to make ready to excuse myself. In the African milieu, leaving is a protracted process. They make Ents and Midwestern Lutherans look hasty. Ken's wife, Meli, invited us to eat lunch with them and their family of ten adopted children. Dani looked at me imploringly. She knew the reputation of Madame Johnson's table.

I accepted for both of us, and we washed hands with the little kids and were seated at the head of the main table. The fish and chips were hot and tasty Lake Tanganyika sangala–pink, like salmon. The vegetable salad was dressed with a rich cheese sauce. The conversation was delightful. The household was peaceful and happy and busy. We were deeply blessed. After seconds, the dishes were cleared and I started to make noises about leaving again. Meli said "What about a piece of chocolate cake and a cup of coffee?"

I had been on simple Burundian rations for a month. Spartans don't do sauce. Klingons don't bake cake. I almost wept. Dani laughed and accepted for me. When the last molecule of cake was gone, we both expressed deep appreciation again.

Then, Mr. Ken Johnson brought out two lime green fluorescent safety vests. Mr. Ken Johnson is a great believer in safety. Dani and I met eyes and smiled. Fashionistas, the both of us, we knew we were wearing our new coats home. We donned our gear with as much dignity as green fluorescent allows.

More gratitude and a walk out to the bike to discover that she had acquired two more blinking lights taped on with green fluorescent tape to her front and another to the back. God grinned–both of them. Mr. Ken Johnson was pleased. One of the little boys said, "You look like the president's escort!" And so we did. The escort of some president in a Doctor Seuss story.

After more admiration and gratitude, Milagro leapt to a run and we drove home. The stares and gestures of the last few weeks were raised by a magnitude of ten. We were officially a spectacle. I was about halfway home when I started laughing. Dressed and fed and cared for by the grace of God, for our wellbeing and joy. Visible like a city on the hill. Letting our lights shine. So visible that Dani's comment upon disembarking was, "Well, if they kill us now on the road, it will be murder!"

Service

One morning I was heading downtown to David's office without Dani. I was on one of the feeder routes from the suburbs, but not one where most of the moto-boys stationed themselves. It can be a little hard to get a taxi, car or moto, on that route. So when the very well-dressed Burundian gentleman spotted my bike, he was relieved. He waved me the universal "come-hither" motion to call the taxi. He was not paying a lot of attention to anything except his fancy watch.

I could not resist. When I came to a stop, I said, "Good Morning, Monsieur! Where do you need to go?" He jumped back at my English and my face. Then he laughed and looked about—they have prank-TV shows in Africa too.

He said, in beautiful English, "But seriously! Who are you?"

"I am Madame Moto-Muzungu, riding this morning for American Motos. And it is your lucky day! All rides are free today! But soon we will be charging double for riding behind beautiful American ladies."

He thought it was a great business plan. He was bound for a conference at the Novotel. He arrived on time, with no damage to his beautiful suit. And a story that no one was going to believe.

I consider it my spiritual duty to mess with people's heads. God does it so often with me, that I figure that as one of God's agents in the world, it should be one of my primary activities. You cannot be mean with it. You must always leave them with the impression that something weird and wonderful has just occurred. If you live your life in such a way that people are always wishing for witnesses to corroborate their testimony, you are doing it right.

Subversion—Shopping Edition

One of our favorite subversive moto games was shopping downtown. Certain types of shopping I never did, because the prices tripled when I showed my face. So Dani did my purchasing for me. This allowed us to act out a wonderful charade on the local stage.

It was odd for me to be on the moto–that, we have well established. But Daniella presented them with a whole different conundrum, and the conundrum that was Dani is not as well-plumbed.

The moto boys were pretty sure that I was not a commercial enterprise. But, sometimes they wondered. They had seen different people on my pillion. The back seat is the seat of the purchaser, the usual power position. But white is power, and old is power, and we subverted both those paradigms when Dani is behind me. It confused them.

We compounded this when we shopped. I would ride up to the moto stand and discharge Dani, then pull into line with the rest of the boys. She would hand me her helmet and say in nice Kirundi, "Please wait, I won't be long." I would say "*Oui, Mademoiselle.*" They were confounded. They tried to quiz me, but I have almost no Kirundi. Well, I can say, "*Sindabizi Ikirundi*" which means, "I can't speak Kirundi" in Kirundi. Their puzzlers were puzzed.

I would twiddle my thumbs and watch traffic with them. When Dani came back with her packages, I would say, "*Iko Wapi?*" "Where to?" in Kiswahili. She replied, "Home, please," in her nice French and I said "OK" in universal, and I grinned at the boys, and off we went.

"Who IS that GIRL????"
"How does she rate a lady *muzungu* driver??"
"Maybe she is the daughter of the president?"
"Don't be stupid! There would be guns!"
"True."
And the boys would have something to think about all afternoon.

Celebrity

For about six weeks, I was a celebrity. Being a white woman walking around downtown Buja still makes you unusual, but it is no longer a rarity. If you are a white woman driving her own car, you are a bit more rarefied, because all the white women working for the NGO's have drivers. But middle class Burundian women now drive, so you don't get too many looks. But a white woman, riding a moto, with a beautiful Burundian girl sidekick, in matching green fluorescent vests on a shiny new red bike equipped with strobe lights–well, you are officially a spectacle. You are memorable. You are clearly superheroes. You not only get looked at and pointed at, you get cheers from the sidewalks, and you become the answer to the dinner table question, "Well, what did you see in town today?"

But as with anything new and brave, the reaction wasn't completely unmixed. It was about 65% Hosannas, 20% incredulity and the other 15% considered us to be an abomination to God and an insult to African manhood–especially that part of mankind that would never own a moto, and so resented us. Traditional Burundian culture is very hierarchical and patriarchal. At the dinner table, Papa eats first, and then Mama, and then the children get what is left. Motos, even bicycles, represent wealth and power. Most of the men I knew thought we were a great deal of fun, but women and girls on motos driving past men who have nothing but feet may be seen as an affront.

There is always a part of the crowd that wants to see you fail. I couldn't always tell the difference. On one of my regular shortcuts, there was a beer hall on the street and the men there always greeted me with a distinctive call. I always smiled and waved.

Kama Kawaide, it was up to Dani to educate me.

"Peggy, those men are not cheering for you."

"Really? They seem friendly."

"They are drunk. And they are ex-rebels."

"How do you know that?"

"Because that noise they are making is their battle cry—it is what you hear coming from the bush before they come to kill you."

"Ah. Do you think they plan to kill me?"

"Probably not. They want to scare you, and make you crash the bike; then they would laugh, and maybe steal the bike, and maybe..."

Better informed, I developed my own version of a rebel yell to give back to them; they threw a few pebbles at us, but eyes on the road, Milagro never faltered.

The cadre of fellow moto riders was much more supportive. They understand solidarity. On about my third day, they accepted me, and I rode as one of their own until the end. It was they who named me "Madame Moto-Muzungu."

One day, on one of the terrifyingly complex roundabouts, at the height of morning rush hour, a moto stalled mid-stream. Death. The swarm that I was a part of surrounded our comrade and stopped en masse, raised our throttle hands, and shouted in Kirundi. Can't kill us all (probably). Traffic stopped, and we escorted the man and moto safely to the side of the road. An ad hoc repair committee was formed and the rest of us rode on our way. *Hakuna Matata*—it's just what we do.

By the end of the six weeks, I was well known, and I recognized many of them as individuals. Be-beeps of greeting in the morning and at night. They work 12 hour shifts six days a week. I was more irregular, but always welcomed.

Then my time ran out. I wanted to arrange an escort to accompany Milagro back to Miracle Motors, but with little functional Kirundi, I did not know how. So with an escort of angels, we quietly surrendered our steed. I did sing the doxology at the top of my lungs for the final three blocks. Dani was humiliated. Mr. Muni Raju was out to lunch, so I wrote a thank-you note and gave the key and helmets to the secretary, and walked away, Lone Ranger-style. I did leave the deepest blessing I knew how to give, on the bike and the man who would become her new master, though I knew him not. Then I adjusted my African explorer hat and became a foot soldier again.

I took a regular taxi home. The car taxi men are a union all their own, and also very tight. They pride themselves on a knowledge of the town and its goings-on that would make a London cabbie blush with shame. This man kept sneaking hard looks at me in the mirror. Finally he said, "Why are you in my cab, Madame? Where is your moto? You are the one? No? Madame Moto-Muzungu?" I explained that I was on my way to America and that the moto would stay. "*Ai*! This is a sad day for the moto boys."

The next day, I was downtown with Dani. We walked past the biggest moto stand in the core. I smiled and *bonjour*ed the boys, but not a one of them acknowledged me. They did not recognize me without the helmet and bike and vest. I was once again just some old white woman.

Sigh. Fame is so fleeting.

I understood in a new way, "He came into His own country—to his own people—and they did not recognize Him."

Petit Epilogue:

She is gone. We do not know where she went, but then we did not know where she came from. She was with us for such a short season. But when she was here, we shined.

The boys on the south end of town say she lived in Kibenga, and that she came to them first, and they claimed her, but they do not know which compound she went into at night, nor where she is now.

The boys in Kamenge say that she was a teacher and pastor and went every day to the church to teach. But that is ridiculous; no church would let a *muzungu* lady-pastor ride a moto! Those boys drink too much beer.

Those bad men in Bwiza were seen throwing stones at her and trying to frighten her. But she was fearless, and if they had gotten her we would have heard about that. She would not run from men like that.

A taxi man claims that she rode with him and has gone to America. But you cannot trust taxi-men. A downtown boy claims to know the girl who rode with her, but the girl denies that she has ever worn the beautiful green vest. Someone asked Mr. Kenny Johnson, and he smiled and said he was sure she would return some day. We can only hope.

But she is gone, and the days are less bright, and the rains have come.

Part 6: Off The Grid

The cool thing that happens after you accept the fact that nothing is ever safe, is that you come to the realization that you were never in any danger. It's not that the whole thing was a dream, it wasn't—flying monkeys are very real. It's just that the flying monkeys and the Cyclops never had the power to hurt you. You weren't lost, you were wearing the sparkly shoes the whole time. Bitchy goddesses are all green smoke and bluster. You were sent here complete and whole, everything you could need is somewhere around this place. You will be fine if they don't like you. You will be fine if they don't believe you. You will be fine when you get your exit visa stamped.

But sometimes we forget.

Fresh Roads

When I got my first motorcycle, one of the first things I did was go down to the State Department of Transportation and buy the big map of the county that I live in. It was several feet to a side and showed every road and alley within about 30 miles of my house. I started marking off each road as I covered it. Soon I had to purchase the maps for the five counties around my county. Now my map took up a whole wall of my house and I had fresh road in every direction of me. After ten years and two bikes, it became harder to find fresh road in the State of Oregon; and Oregon is about 350 miles tall by 400 miles wide.

So, sometime after the turn of the century, I was offered a preaching gig in Idaho and decided to take the opportunity to knock off some out-of-the-way roads in the very far northeastern corner of Oregon.

Perhaps you do not fully understand why fresh road is so important. There is nothing that prevents the miracle in your back yard. There is nothing that even slows down sister Serendipity from meeting you at the corner grocery store, if she is looking for you. The Kingdom of Heaven is within you and can erupt at any time. However, the major inhibitor of that eruption is your own soul sleepiness. It is way too easy to get stuck on spiritual cruise control. Common intimacy encourages entropy.

The best way I know to break out of this is to find fresh road. I do it quite literally. Riding a road where I do not know what is around the next corner requires a level of awareness that makes me feel very lively. I have to pay attention. I cannot daydream.

I know people who can find fresh road in a laboratory that they walk into every day for years. I know people who find fresh road on a blank piece of paper, or on the well-known strings of their favorite guitar.

Still, I like the wind. The unpredictability of the weather. So I was up in the country of Chief Joseph of the Nez Perce. His precious blue lake is still there. The appaloosa descendants of his favorite ride live and eat this year's grass. His Spirit and the Spirit of his people flow down off those mountains towards the Snake River.

I reached the edge of the Snake after a long descent down the backside of the Wallowa Mountains on an unpaved road. I had been counting on a bridge over a dam on the map. The dam was there, but it was no bridge. So like Joseph, I turned north towards Canada and several hundred miles out of my way. Unlike Joseph, my steed could not eat grass. At least there was no cavalry at my back. My limits were the limits of a gas tank, not how far you could push the elders carrying the babies on their backs. I wasn't worried, because although the ranch houses were few and far between at that point, I knew that ranch people kept a fill of gas cans and kindness, and the worst I could face was a walk or a wait. I talked to God, and to Joseph, and to the Appies in the fields.

And just after I had switched my fuel valve over to 'reserve', meaning that I had less than a quart left of petrol, I saw a boy of about twelve, walking.

"Hi, Lady." Blonde hair, freckles, big tooth smile. Huck Finn.

"Son, I need some gasoline and I need it pretty soon. How much trouble am I in?"

"Well, I wouldn't know about trouble, but if you take that next gravel road up there, you can cut through to the road that goes to the place where my dad takes his coffee. Mrs. Wright, she has a pump in the back–you might have to ask."

"Thanks. Really, I mean it. Do you need a ride, son?"

"No, ma'am, my Ma would switch my butt if I got caught takin' a ride with no helmet. Ma's pretty strict about the helmets. I don't have far to go."

"Sorry I don't have a spare, son. You take care."

"Bye, Lady—oh, and the pie's really good—have the peach, if she has any left."

The peach pie was fabulous. The shortcut got me there in less than ten miles. Mrs. Wright did indeed have a small reserve of gasoline. I described the boy to Mrs. Wright and the ranchers taking their coffee. I was hoping to speak a good word about him and his manners to someone who knew him. Maybe leave him a small reward—though I doubted any adult would convey a reward to a boy for just being neighborly, as they would expect such.

Mrs. Wright and all the ranchers were of one mind that there was no such boy of that description or even of that age living on any ranch within 40 miles of that diner. They said they knew by name every child within that distance. I believed them.

I did another hundred miles of fresh road that day. Wide awake.

Mechanical Failure

Life for Rosie requires three things; air, fuel and a spark. Air and fuel are both chemical. She sucks air in through her filters. I am pretty sure it is the oxygen part that goes "Boom" with the fuel. Fuel is dead dinosaur dirty. Fuel stinks and makes stink. Rosie accepts this as the messy necessity of life. Rosie has a carburetor, a choke and a mixture screw. This combo is a mechanical device with two manual controls that mix air with fuel. The mix must be just right. Rich on fuel to start, then more air-less fuel. There is a default setting, correct for here at sea level. When we get above 8,000, feet she starts to wheeze and complain and the screw must be adjusted to change the mix.

Air is still mostly free. Fuel is not cheap but we get 40-50 miles per gallon. When we were young, that was way better than any car, but we've been losing our bragging rights on that count. Four citizens in a Prius is way more economical, but we don't care. We skipped economics class.

The spark is a whole different thing. It is the mysterium of the process. Rosie has a traveling alchemy box that transforms liquid and metal chemistry into electricity, but she only uses that for starting. The rest of the time the spark is supplied by a mechanical device that turns motion into electricity using a magnetic coil. I am pretty sure this is sorcery. This trinity of ether, body and lightning combine to create the fire of life.

She and I are two of a kind in this matter. I am a combination of a lot of carbon-based stink, plus some oxygen and a spark of something quite different. We understand each other. We both understand that the mix is holy and that the mix can get out of whack.

Mechanical creatures have flaws, weaknesses, and besetting sins just like organic creatures. Some problems come with the particular breed, some are idiosyncratic. Rosie doesn't always breathe right. When she does, there is a little whistle through the tank lock. Bill, my mechanic, says that a whistling bike is a happy bike. When she doesn't breathe right, she seals herself up too tight and creates a vacuum in her tank and then the gas can't flow. Yet she can run a ridiculously long time all locked up like that. Time enough to get down the freeway or into the desert. This is her besetting sin. I know this about her. I have done things to mitigate it. It is scary when it happens at speed in the left lane of the interstate. But I know what to do, and it always works. I forgive her every time.

It is no different for me. A strong physical body and a divine spark are not enough if I lock myself all up—if I stop inhaling and exhaling. My life is not my own; it depends on sources beyond myself. I have to relax and take in as I let go. Breathe as I burn, or I shall become a dead organic paperweight as surely as my steel steed. What seems odd is that my own besetting sins so often catch me by surprise.

Sudden mechanical failure is a different animal and always feels like betrayal. It's not, of course. There is always a logical, not an emotional cause. And it is rare that it is actually sudden. It's just that at some point it becomes news to the rider. The bike saw it coming. Machines break, sometimes at the very wrong time. Good maintenance attempts to replace things before they snap. But this does not always work.

We were on the way down the west slope of the Cascades towards the barn. I had ridden a thousand miles in three days. I was ready to be home. The September sun was just setting as Salem came into view and the Golden Pioneer on top of the State Capitol was catching the light like an Olympian god. Rosie had been running like a champ. When I was eight blocks from the house, I saw the last traffic light turn yellow. I could have run it, but I decided to not push my luck at the end of a good ride and stopped.

So did Rosie. I figured my wearied foot had downshifted poorly and I had killed her engine. When I tried to re-start her, she made no noise whatsoever. She did not try and turn over. She did not respond in any way. I was exhausted and sure I was doing something stupid. I called home. Alivia jumped in the car and came over. I was sure she would be able to make her go. No such luck. Rocinante was a 500-pound paperweight. I was too tired to push her home. She rode the last mile on the back of a tow truck. When Bill got her, he knew it was the alternator—the magic part. If the alternator fails, you have only as much time as it takes to drain the battery before you lose the spark and the engine dies and then you roll only as far as gravity will take you. Rosie's alternator had a catastrophic failure. No particular cause, it could have happened anywhere on that thousand mile trip—out in the middle of nowhere. If the light had been green, she would have made it. As it was, she got me within easy reach of the barn and help before she gave up the ghost. How do you not feel loyalty for that?

Forest Fires

If you are out in the middle of God's Country, anywhere west of the Mississippi, and you have the sudden awareness that the next ridge over is shrouded in a level of smog that only Los Angeles could produce, and you are nowhere near that fabled Babylon, it is good to stop and get some local advice. You are likely looking at a forest fire.

I have ridden through three forest fires. The most spectacular of them was in the Umpqua National Forest in southern Oregon. I was coming down from Crater Lake. The road follows the Umpqua River and is a curvy and beautiful canyon.

Just about the time that I saw the smoke, I saw a state trooper parked in the middle of the road. He had a short line of cars stopped. I joined the queue. The word was that there was a fast moving fire about 20 miles down and while it was not yet near the road, they were worried about the winds. He was waiting for word as to whether the road would be opened or closed for the day. We waited with him.

Forest fires are sneaky and fast. In dry country, they can jump roads, rivers and ridges. The people fighting them have enough problems; they don't need to let random tourists get too close. A couple of cars turned and headed back up and over the Cascades to better chances. My problem was that I had come far enough down that I had used just better than half my gas. I had enough to go forward to the town at the bottom of the canyon, but not quite enough to get back to where I had come from.

I conferred with the trooper, he grokked my situation, and advised me to hang a bit, as he thought the winds were going to push the fire away from the road, not near it. If I had to turn around, he would siphon me a bit of fuel. Half an hour later, the word came that winds were from the southwest and favorable. He was authorized to open the road for 30 minutes.

He looked me up and down. "You good for this?"

"Sure," I said.

"Might be smarter to take some gas and head back up."

"I have this thing about turning around–and my mileage is great downhill."

"Okay. Go first, go fast, don't stop for anything, And no matter what happens, DO NOT leave the road."

I took off. There were a couple hours of daylight left. I was going westward and down. The winds were in my face or to my left. The river was on my left with ridges of various heights to my right. The first 30 minutes were beautiful, lonely and clear. They didn't seem to be letting anyone start up the road. Then I noticed smog up and off to my right but not close. The sky got brown and hazy, but high up. I still felt like I had this.

Then the winds shifted. There were oven-hot downdrafts coming off the ridge to my right. I was in a tight canyon section of the river valley. I knew I was not more than ten miles from where it would open back out into greener farmland. I cranked the throttle and concentrated on the yellow line. The sky got suddenly darker, the road took a left hand bend and I looked up to see flames at the top of the ridge in front of me, licking into the air like a punk rocker's Mohawk. It started to rain ash.

Even my hellfire and brimstone childhood had not prepared me for this kind of apocalypse. The sun was lowering blood red into a brown cloud in front of me. But there was nothing to do but move. In my helmet, I was skipping the angels and talking straight to Jesus. Just when my nerves were starting to fray, the canyon opened out, and a cool breeze blew up from the southwest, and I knew I was done.

When I got to the first gas station, I stopped to fill and gather my wits.

"Geez. Did you just come down?" asked the pump kid. "See the fire?"

"Yeah, it was a bit harrowing."

"They closed the road both ways just about an hour ago."

"Trooper sent me through, but I didn't see anyone behind or before me."

"Well, some days you just get away with it, don't you?"

My Burundian friends have this view of death. They believe that if it is not your day to die that nothing can hurt you, and that if it is your day to die, nothing can save you. It is a pretty good philosophy for doing you daily business in a war zone. It is possible that I picked up a bit too much of that virus. It is also possible that they are right.

Gas Anxiety

I don't know why I do it. But I often pass my last best chance for gas.

Port Orford, Oregon, is so beautiful it looks photo shopped. Rocky coastal bay, deep green forest, pushing straight down to the cold blue water. "Cold" being as much a central feature as "beautiful." And windy. The locals consider a 30mph wind to be a light breeze. Fifty and steady is not considered a storm.

I stopped there for gas, and worked to stay upright. The wind was 30 with gusts of 50. The gas-man thought it was a great day because it was sunny. Sunny may be something they don't see all that often. The annual rainfall is about six foot two.

I had been riding south all morning with an ambient temp in the low 60's. With wind chill, I was freezing. I decided to cross the California border and then turn inland, cutting off the tip of the redwoods to scoot back up into Oregon and up to a town called Cave Junction.

Port Orford to Cave Junction is 124 miles. Rosie's tank is good for 120 miles with neutral winds. The winds were not neutral. The last good-sized town I would go through was Brookings. When I got there, I still had a half tank.

Good sense says that I should have stopped to top off. But good sense is not my strong suit. I was pretty sure that there was gas in a hamlet halfway between the big trees and Cave Junction called Gasquet, which they locals pronounce Gas-Key. At least there was the last time I rode through, about a decade ago.

Thirty miles after Brookings, I passed a perfectly good gas pump at Haiuchi, CA. I have no explanation for my behavior. It's about refusing to slow down. It's about thinking that I know where I am going. It's about thinking there is some kind of moral benefit to stretching my resources to their absolute limit. It is stupid. I know it. So does my inner Jiminy Cricket, who as I passed said, "I think you should have stopped." If Rosie had a voice, I am sure she would have agreed with my conscience. But I rolled on, and then the pump at Gasquet was closed. I had enough to get back to Haiuchi, but I am positively allergic to going backwards. So I backed her off down to 55, coasted on any declines and sat with my gas anxiety.

I hate gas anxiety. It sours the stomach. But clearly, I do not hate it enough to develop sensible refueling habits. Rosie asked for her reserve switch about 14 miles from Cave Junction and just as the forest fire I had not heard about made itself clear over the next ridge. Forest fires do not improve gas anxiety. At that point, I did not have enough gas to get anywhere but forward. Rosie has about a quart of petrol on reserve, good for about 10 miles.

At the near suburb of Cave Junction, a hamlet named O'Brien, there is fuel. I made it. Perhaps I need to consider the possibility that I am a wee bit addicted to the feeling of relief that comes after the peril. It is my only theory. But the joy of the near-miss settles me down. A good-sized near-miss can make me prudent for months afterwards.

An O'Brianite told me that the fire was near Grants Pass, a town that knows no apostrophes and is often referred to as Grass Pants. It was directly on my route, but they said it had not closed any roads yet. I parked in Grants Pass for the night with ash fall and spooky firelight over the ridge to the north—very apocalyptic. I slept like the righteous dead.

Imprudent resource management gets men killed during forest fires. I don't do this financially, or in any other area of my life. I consider it to be one of my motorcycle-specific besetting sins. It is unfortunate that Rosie and I have a dysfunctionally-matched set of besetting sins, especially since if I got over mine and opened her tank more often, her problem would be lessened.

I know other couples with perfectly matched problems. And I see the ruin of badly managed self-care all the time. It is one of the big issues of our culture and day. Not knowing when to stop. Not listening to that still small voice that speaks wisdom. The Master said that we were supposed to take care of others like we watch over ourselves. I don't think He meant badly.

Chick Bike

I was in Burns, Oregon, early on day two of my annual get -off-the-grid retreat. This one was also an Ironbutt. Ironbutt is one of the basic motorcycle traditions, or spiritual disciplines, if you will, where you try and do as many miles as possible, as many days as you can, in a row. In a serious competitive Ironbutt, they do a thousand miles in 24 hours, or Atlantic to Pacific in 50. It is the triathlon for bikes. My best is 650 in one day, or 1500 in three. There is something in the human spirit, well, in some humans at least, that wants to find out what the terminal limits of strength and endurance are. I am no Diana Nyad, but I have the itch and an understanding of the full disease.

Burns is at the dead center of the state of Oregon. It is high desert. It freezes in the winter (and some summer nights) and blazes on the summer days. There are Basque shepherds out there—strong people. Don't know what they left in Spain to make Burns look like heaven—the Inquisition, I figure.

I stopped in early at the grocery to get some supplies, as I expected to be in lonely country for most of the day. As I was loading my provender in my pack, a big ranch truck pulled up. A large man and a small boy got out. The son was about four, and was sporting a black pseudo-Stetson that he would not grow into before puberty. Father tipped his summer straw at me.

"Ma'am."

"G'day, sir"

Son stopped, planted his feet wide, crossed his arms and stared at me.

"Hey, little cowboy."

Father stopped. "Son, you know how to say hello, don't you?"

" 'Low ma'am, I like your motorcycle. Gonna get me one of those someday."

"You do that, little fella."

"Come along, Son."

I like how in ranch country they train children to talk to strangers.

I also stopped in to top off the tank. There are stretches in every direction from Burns where you can go a hundred miles or better without any chance at gas. There are stretches of a hundred miles where you see no sign of human habitation. Rosie's three gallons were augmented with the bungeed spare can.

At the Petrol Emporium, there were two Good Old Boys on Honda Goldwings, sitting off to the side watching traffic. I could see them note my arrival with words, but their faces cracked with grins when I took off my helmet.

GOB #1 walked up to me.

"This is so funny! When you rolled in, Bob here said to me, 'That's the perfect Chick bike!' and then here you are, an actual chick!"

He wanted me to laugh with him. I failed to see the funny.

See, let me unpack this...

They thought their bikes were cooler than mine.

They thought I was a dude, and the best put-down of my bike was to call it a chick bike.

If I had been a dude, they would have kept that to themselves.

Since I was female, they pronounced themselves witty and wanted me to share and admire their wit. They presumed I would not be insulted to have my steed labeled "Pretty good for a girl."

I ignored the wit and made a tangential remark about Rosie's faithfulness and why I think that 750 cc's is the perfect size for about anyone.

GOB said "Well, a man like me would look like a dog trying to ride a flea on something that little." I didn't see anything particularly big about him except for his gut and his ego.

I looked over at his bike.

"Those are real pretty rigs you have there—I didn't know Winnebago was making bikes, but they seem to be doing a good job of it. Have a good day!"

They were just GOBs. They didn't mean no harm. They had no power to put a dent in my joy or freedom. But I wonder where, between the awestruck cowpoke stage and the oblivious GOB stage, some boys/men tip from respect to derision. I wonder if, and if so how, we will ever get to a place where "female", in all its forms, is no longer used as an insult.

It's a story as old as Eve. Which I think is a pretty interesting story and pert near true. It is a story about forgetting who you really are, and letting distrust turn into brokenness and the rule of fear. But the lesson has been missed for millennia. And the story has been used to blame and abuse woman and all her daughters. To turn her beauty into an insult. To deny her strength and power. But those who use it that way have forgotten the ending. Woman is tasked with the eradication of vermin in all its forms, and she is promised victory.

Begging

Hwy 95 runs along the Oregon/Idaho border, north-south. I was headed south towards Winnemucca, Nevada. I didn't intend to go all that way—I have no use for the state of Nevada, but I wanted to move a latitude or two, equatorwise. The road goes first through irrigated farm country and then out into rolling dry lands. It was warm and beautiful. There was quite a bit of traffic, so I just settled in. I did not care to pass with care.

I can only conclude that the coyote was suicidal. We were on a flat stretch with thousands of acres of nothing in every direction. It was mid-morning and visibility was perfect when the coyote jumped up from the ditch and threw himself in front of the eighteen wheeler right in front of me. I guess he had taken all he could take of that roadrunner. The eighteen wheels chewed that dog up something fierce and spit it up and out the back—right at my windscreen.

If the object flying at your bike is smaller than a deer, and not as hard as a piece of lumber, you will probably survive the impact. Panicked avoidance and over-correction will kill you more often. I saw it coming and shifted just a little off center and shut my eyes—just try and stop that reaction. Coyote bits glanced off my starboard side. Yuck. But nothing worse than that. I did not see any reason to stop.

The plan for the day was to go through Jordan Valley, Rome, and then turn Northeast at Burns Junction and head back towards Burns. By the map, it looked like there would be gas in Jordan Valley and Burns Junction.

When I pulled into Jordan Valley, the state police had the entire road stopped. The town had no stoplights and one sharp bend. I was back in Basque country. Turns out I arrived on the actual one hundredth birthday of the town, and right in time for the parade.

The Basques, the cowboys and the First Peoples were all out and having a feast day. I saw a three year-old boy riding a 15-hand horse and nobody thought it was amazing except me. And John Dillinger apparently wasn't killed in Chicago, 'cause I saw him driving in the parade in a '32 Packard. The gendarme held us back until the main body passed, but then we were free to join it. I love me a parade, even if it does mean riding through a great deal of horse shit.

Sadly, very sadly, I did not have time to wait for the sheep that the Basques had in the ground pit to roast all day, and the matriarchs were just heating the oil for the fry bread. Lord knows, I know better than to pester or push a matriarch, so I rolled into the Jordan Valley Cafe for a little late breakfast. I figured no one there was going to be bothered by the coyote or horse splatter on my pants.

The Jordan Valley Cafe is small. I walked in the front door and had the eyes of everyone in the room, on Centennial Saturday, the busiest day in a long time. That was 18 eyes. Not sets—eyes.

The Basque wife raised her eyebrows at me and went back to her eggs and husband. A straw-hatted rancher smiled and said hello. The waitress told me to sit wherever I wanted. There was only one free spot. That's what I wanted.

She bustled over in a couple of minutes with two waters, coffee, and two menus.

"It's just me." I said.

"Where's the fellow you came in with?"

"Hmm, if you can see my imaginary friend then I guess we are both in trouble."

The room laughed.

The waitress squint-eyed me with suspicion, looking about for the other fellow. She left the second water. It turns out they will let you have huckleberry ice cream on your French toast at the Jordan Cafe and serve it up with thick fresh bacon. I didn't order anything for my friend.

Before I left, I checked my directions with Straw Hat. I told him how I planned to get back to Burns. He said it would work. He asked me if I was carrying water with me. I was. I should have asked him about gas, but I was feelin' good about my bungeed reserve can. I "Fair-thee-welled" the room and was waved and "Ride carefull'd" on my way.

I left town to the West. I felt eyes on me as I did. I had to pass an actual stagecoach leaving from the parade.

It was about 50 miles from Jordan Valley to Burns Junction. About a hundred up to Burns from there. That would require 47 mpg, and I hadn't been getting that in any kind of wind. I passed through Rome at mile 30, counting on a rightly placed one-pump wonder at the Junction. Badly weathered signs promised gas and a cafe. All signs out there are badly weathered. There isn't really any other kind of weather. When I got to the junction of 95 and 78 north, it was clear that no one had been pumping gas or cutting pies there in years. I was not yet worried.

Then the road started to gain altitude. This is the east side of the Steens–The Sheephead Mountains to be specific. The wind kicked up. I tried to keep the smartest and steadiest speed. I talked to Rosie and Jesus, and the angels. No one but me seemed worried. It was BLM lands. All the kinds of nothin'. But it was beautiful and tolerably cool and I was singing most of the way. At one panoramic wide spot, I stopped and put the bungeed gas in the main tank. I congratulated myself on my smarts.

I hadn't seen a vehicle in either direction for over half an hour, so I peed right there by the side of the road. There was no plant life to offer any cover, but none was needed. I was very alone. It was so dry out there that squatting eight inches off the ground the stream evaporated before hitting dirt.

I enjoyed the hours going north. There was some nice geology and at one point I stopped to get a lava rock for the wall I am building in my yard. I had a spare helmet bungeed up on top, and the can behind, so not much room for adding boulders. The helmet had ridden along because I was wearing a brand new one, and sometimes they hurt a bit when new, but this one had been just great, and the old one was fairly shot... so... I impaled my spare lid on a barbed wire fence post and put the rock up on top of my pack behind my head. I imagined people driving by, wondering about that helmet all winter. Maybe they will make up stories. One can only hope.

Okay, so maybe adding a heavy boulder didn't help my gas mileage. And maybe putting it up on top of the pack behind my head wasn't all that smart. "No sudden stops, girl, or you are gonna be killed by your own luggage..." Someone whispered.

But I felt I was within reach of Burns. Then just as I was coming back into ranch country, the sputter, the twist, the warning. Then ten miles on reserve, and I was still 17 out from Burns. And I started looking at ranches for friendliness.

Then she stopped. Nice and close to a lane that went up to a good-looking ranch house. I got the spare can from the back and hiked up that lane. The sight of a four-wheeler in a pick-up truck was a good omen. The fact that the pick-up was labeled Law Enforcement–Search and Rescue was even better. Now all I needed was someone home. An ancient brown hunting dog met me, tail-a-waggin', and escorted me to the kitchen door. I knocked.

Fine lookin' man comes to the door and smiles.

"How you doing?

I hold up the can.

"I've had better days, but I have had many worse ones. I guess I'm about as good as a dry woman can be."

"I'll put on a shirt and we'll see what I can do about that."

His name was John and the place is the Lazy J just outside of Crane.

It is a good thing to occasionally be at the utter end of your resources and have no solution except for human kindness. It is good to have nothing to offer but a handshake and a promise of a prayer.

Sometimes... Jesus pays my bills.

He pays at a higher rate than I do too.

I hope John gets ten times what he deserves.

Lost

Once in a while, if I am good at getting off the grid, and if I am lucky enough to be on fresh roads, I get good and lost. Not only does no one else in the world know where I am, but neither do I. Living in the western part of the United States helps with this. There is more room to get lost.

One time, I was out in Eastern Oregon, and I made a couple of unusual turns and ended up on a long stretch of unpaved road. I went about 50 miles without pavement and without seeing anything but trees. Then I realized that the sun was in the wrong quadrant of the sky. Hmm—I usually have a good internal compass—this was confusing.

But most roads come out somewhere. And eventually, pavement returned and then I rolled into a small logging town. It had a gas station/café—Hallelujah! I decided to dig down to the bottom of the pack for that map. I went into the café and spotted the oldest man in the place.

"Good morning, sir!" I chirped

"Mornin," he said, supplying the stock laconic response.

"I've got a map here, would you be so kind as to point out exactly where we are. I am still in Oregon, right?"

I so treasured the look on his face when he dropped jaw.

"You don't know where you are?"

"Not the foggiest idea. Ain't that great?—I'm on vacation!"

He put a crooked, dented old finger on the map for me.

"Wow, I am totally off my non-course. This is going to be interesting."

Like most people, I hate being lost when I am late to a specific spot at a specific time. I get annoyed when I am trying to achieve a specific destination and I am failing. But even then, I almost always learn things as I take a severely alternative route to my destination. Psychologists call this latent learning, picking things up as you go. Of course, it only works if you are paying attention, and when your anxiety is low enough for you to encode new information. Sometimes I get to travel at 100% latent learning level. Lost can be fun.

Now, I have to admit that I am using the term lost loosely. I don't believe much in the concept of lost. Not physically, not theologically. I always know what planet I am on, and what continent, and which country, and usually what state. The rest is fine-tuning. I may be in need of direction, or of a gas station or of a bed, but I am okay, just temporarily displaced. And God and the angels always know where I am.

Some people think that souls can be lost. This is nonsensical to me. That spark of Spirit in me, that connects me beyond dimensional space to all that is good, is placed precisely where it was placed when I began. It will be there until a process beyond my control sucks it back out of this body and this dimension to that great someplace else. That spark is not much affected by my whims or hormones or physical circumstance.

By lost, of course, some people mean damned. Spiritually wrong to the point of utter disconnect from God. My own experience with attempted apostasy does not actually bear this out. It is so obvious to me that God moved not one nano-bit away from me during my intentional god-hiatus. My spark did not go out, nor do I believe it was in any danger during that time. If anything, the universe started to arrange itself for my good and protection during that time. I did nothing to cooperate with that process, but I can see it in hindsight. The universe still had me on a path to Salvation.

Here's how I think about Salvation. It is like a peach pit. The pit has encoded within it everything it needs to know to become a peach tree. It cannot become an apple tree. There is nothing wrong with the seed in its dormant state. It is perfect, complete and everything it is supposed to be as a seed. Yet, it is not a producing peach tree. And it is in great need of external help to become that tree.

This is a Quaker view of the human condition—NOT ruined, depraved or necessarily even fallen, but valuable and invested with life and a plan even in the simplest stages. This is the view of humanity that we see in the first chapter of John—life and light in everyone born, but still in need of Divine visitation and assistance.

In addition to time, the seed needs at least two things to become a producing tree. The first is to be planted and watered, which will allow the seed to be germinated and awakened. This awakening is programmed into the seed—the seed wants to germinate, and yet it will not happen until the conditions are right. This can happen by fortuitously falling to the right place on the ground at the right time, or it can happen with the help of a tree grower who intentionally plants and waters the seed.

This is the process that Jesus refers to when he speaks with Nicodemus. This is the second birth that has become the clichéd "Born-again." The truth that we see here is that there are two births of the peach—the original pollination of the flower that produces the fruit that produces the seed, and the awakening of that seed in germination. And both of those awakenings require some external help and influence. And they both require the grace of God's spark.

So, a soul can't really be lost, it can be nascent—not yet awake. And it can be germinated but stunted. As humans with volition, we can cooperate with that awakening, in ourselves and others, or we can detour it, occasionally deep-freeze it. But awakening is always possible. I cannot fathom a gardener who would punish seeds for being only seeds. Hell is a thing we build out of our own fear. Don't get me wrong, it's real, but it is not God-made or necessary. And I believe with all my heart that it is always temporary.

David, the bad-boy, adulterous, murdering, bi-sexual king prophet said that there was nowhere that we could run from God. That at sea bottom or mountaintop, God is there. David pretty much lived his life proving that one. If he couldn't run far enough, I'm not likely to succeed.

So I don't believe in lost—Just that interesting place that comes right before found.

Not everyone appreciates lost the way I do.

Travis was 25 blocks south when he needed to be ten blocks north. There was not a thing familiar and he knew he was lost. He saw the neon OPEN sign and walked right in to Freedom Friends Church on Sunday morning.

We only do four things at the church on the island of misfit toys. We sing a little, we say thanks, we ask for what we need and we listen. We had just finished gratitudes when the first petition walked in the door.

"I'm sorry to barge in, but I'm looking for North 13th Street and I think this is South 13th, I'm all turned around and don't know how to get where I'm goin'."

He was skinny, sweaty, strung out, and talking Deep South. His ball cap was backwards, his skin was a mess and his belt was pulled tight, holding up the too-big pants.

Our room is an octagon. We sit facing each other. So if you walk in during meeting for worship, all it takes is three steps to be in the middle of the gathering. We continued worship by giving directions. He asked for water; water was given. He was a little frantic at the idea of being so off course. The directions we gave him were clearly not making much sense to him. But eventually, he thanked us for the directions and the drink and went out to retrace his many steps.

We were a small group that day, and all women. I looked at Pastor Alivia and said, "This is safe, right? I'm gonna drive him." She said, "Go." (That's how we do discernment at FFC.)

I followed him out.

"Son!" He turned. "You clean and sober this morning?"

"Yes, Ma'am! Three whole days!"

"You got anything like a weapon on you?"

"No Ma'am! I came up here to get away from all that!"

"Okay, let's get my car. I'll take you where you are going."

"Oh! Thank-you, Ma'am! I 'priciate this, I do!"

He was lately of the State of Mississippi. Came to a cousin's house to start over. I told him my name, and it immediately became Miss Peggy. He was talkin' a mile a minute. "The house numbers kept gettin' bigger—that shoulda been my clue. Somebody told me that golden man there on the capital was solid gold—No?—plate, huh? I figured as much. Say—was that a church meeting I just walked into? Yes? Well, what kinda church IS that?"

I told him we were Quakers. "We don't have much of that down home, Baptists mostly.

But Miss Peggy, if you were willing to leave church to help a lost man find his way, I guess y'all must be some kinda Christians!"

We found his cousin's house. He "God blessed" me up one side and down the other.

"Say a prayer for me, when you get back, ok?" We did.

Vocation

Rosie and I were sitting atop Stinking Water Pass far above the town of Drewsey, Oregon. Across the Caldera from Stinking Water is Drink Water Pass. Drewsey is two miles off of Hwy 20 in the middle of that basin. The whole business is halfway between Burns and the Idaho Border.

My friend Owen's mother, Adeline, was born near Drewsey. I liked his mother. So I left the highway to pay my respects.

We pulled up to the Drewsey Cafe and Gouge Eye Saloon. Sitting on a chair in the sun was a teenage girl, shiny as a new penny. In the shade was a matriarch, sporting flaming red hair and skinning apples. They did not seem surprised to see me.

We exchanged polite morning greetings and I asked if perhaps there was coffee to be had. "She'll pop up and make you some right quick" said the elder. And the girl did pop.

I sat at the worktable and started to try and inquire about Adeline's people, who I knew must be near at hand. I failed. I did not know Adeline's maiden name, only the married one. So I asked after the cause of all the apple peeling.

"Patron of the local school fell under a big ol' bale of hay—he's stove up bad—we're having a fundraiser tonight. I'm makin' a sheet pie."

I expressed my condolences and admiration of the apples. "Gravensteins—my fiancé from over Woodburn way brought them. We're trying a long distance relationship—frankly, it's not workin' and I'm selling this place and movin' to the Valley. I'm too old to wait much."

I allowed as how I taught college two days a week in Woodburn. She said she used to cook for the nuns in Mount Angel. I recalled my days with the nuns taking spiritual direction training. She knew all about spiritual direction. We chatted amiably about our Benedictine friends Antoinette, Dorothy and Jo. "That Jo Morton!—She's a hell of a woman—I tell you!" I agreed wholeheartedly, Jo was my spiritual director for seven years. We laughed at the odds of having such connections.

We talked about vocation. She was educated by the Sisters of Mercy. My new office in Salem is in the old Sisters of Mercy school, I likely sit in the mother superior's space. She asked after my vocation. I admitted to not being a Catholic.

"What's that got to do with it?"

I talked about counseling and trauma healing, teaching psychology and now school administration. She thought I was spread a little bit thin.

"Vocation means doing ONE thing well—I think the sisters taking in women who are grandmothers and widows is bullshit! They are going to end up being half-assed nuns and half-assed grandmothers."

I told her I was trying to BE one thing, even if I was doing many things. She put her apple down and looked at me hard over her half-glasses. She asked me what I was being right now.

I decided to tell her. I leaned in.

"I am completely aware of how close God is to us right now, how the angels are hushed listening to our conversation. I want to live every moment in this unmediated awareness of God, no matter what I am doing."

She sat very still and then said "Well, OK then." She thanked me for stopping in. I thanked her for the spiritual direction—that made her laugh. I told her I would watch for her in Woodburn and wished her good luck with her new fellow.

"Got pie to make—Be safe."

Nose to the Barn

The enemy of the Spiritual Quest is Nose to the Barn Syndrome. NttBS is inevitable, but the spiritual adventurer must seek to keep it at bay until the last possible moment. It occurs in that moment when you stop thinking about the adventure and have eyes only for its end. You tunnel-up your vision and start counting mileposts. Nothing to the left or the right is interesting. You forsake the byways for the straightest of freeways. The only food you want is in your own fridge. You stop for gas only, and that as close to the freeway as possible.

It's not that longing for home and hearth is bad. Sometimes your own bed is heaven. In the last hour of a very good long ride, this determination for home is what will get you there safely. The problem is when NttBS starts too early and robs you of the ride. Weather can do this. Mechanical failure makes it certain. A too-near miss can make you wish for a teleporter. But whatever the cause, the chief result is numb, followed by grim determination. You will not see beauty. You will not see the man in the ditch in need of a Samaritan. You will not be able to turn five miles out of your path to catch something unique and magical.

And some people live their lives this way. Even before mid-life, they are thinking only of a rest ahead. A bad marriage or a crummy job can do this to a person. They think only of how great retirement will be. Or they grimly determine to stick a marriage out, telling themselves that there are no other choices. Depression can give you the syndrome, and the syndrome can leave you depressed. A fixation with suicide is NttBS at its most wicked.

The religion of my childhood had a bad case of NttBS. I spent way too much time as a young child worried about the end of the world. Christendom had looked forward to a triumphant end and Heaven for 1800 years, but with only occasional bouts of obsession with it. Then came an American named John Darby, who, without a computer or even Scotch tape, managed to cut and paste the Book all up to make people believe that he had a roadmap to the Apocalypse. People got all rapture and tribulation crazy and none of it made any sense then or now. It was a bad, bad case of NttBS. There was really no point in life except to prepare for the end and get everyone else to obsess about the preparation with you. It went so nicely with the beginning of the Nuclear age that I was born into, with all its duck-and-cover thinking. But they were wrong. Darby, and the bomb shelter builders, and the whole lot.

I think we are ready for a new way to do Christendom. A way that is more adventurous, a way that puts fear in its rightful place. I think we are ready for some fresh roads, more inclusive and compassionate roads. We need a way of escape that gets us through. I am pretty sure that there will be some wrack and ruin in the process, some things need to be broken open. Some major paradigms need to be subverted. And we have to avoid NttBS. We have to be willing to get off the freeway and investigate the byways and lanes. Some of them will dead end. We have to be willing to turn around. We will have to be open to the voices of strangers to our creeds and codes. We won't make it without a sense of humor and the ability to see beauty in the odd roadside attraction. We will need to stop for pie and conversation.

Much is unknown and cannot be predicted, but I am pretty sure of a short list of things:

1. God is already at work in every single person on this planet. We need to treat people as individuals. We can't exclude a single one, even the problematic ones, maybe especially the problematic ones. We need to help each other out. We need to respect other pathways. We need to listen to each other.

2. Anything we use to mediate the space between ourselves and God will eventually fail, rot, or put us to sleep. The less between you and God the better. We should listen to God, in whatever way God speaks to us.

3. There is a lot of work to do. But we are not alone; saints and angels stand at the ready. There is a lot of adventure to be had doing it.

Sure, there is a barn waiting for all of us. I think I will see my mother and father there. And I bet that bed will feel great. But counting the mileposts won't get you there any faster, and will rob you of the scenery at your shoulder. I plan on staying awake.

EPILOGUE

Ab Aeterno:

"They are rather amazing."

"What? Their capacity for blunder or their persistence in the face of it?"

"They are born so blind. They have no idea what they are, what they are capable of. Whose they are. I mean, someone has to tell them every single thing. But even then, they know nothing until they experience it. It takes some of them years to figure out that they are immortals."

"Many of them never figure that out."

"Well, how can we expect it? Stuck in a linear dimension, and given only a moment. I mean, imagine, to not KNOW, even for a moment."

"Yet they live, and they bear it, and they Love. They reach out into what they don't know and rip Love into their world. They suck the infinite right into the finite. OK. They are amazing."

"I'm glad we have ours."

"She's a piece of work, isn't she?"

"And the bike is fun."

About the Author

Peggy Senger Morrison is a freelance provocateur of grace presently working in the field of education. She is twice a mother and once a grandmother (so far.) Peggy is a Recorded Minister of the Gospel at Freedom Friends Church in Salem, Oregon, and she is married to the talented and beautiful Alivia Biko.

You may contact Peggy through Unction Press at Unction.org.